A Bowl, A Spoon, and a Few Little Miracles

To Oleg
Who helped me
to see things
differently - Ada Warner

How My Family and I Survived Nazi Occupation During WWII

ADEODATA O. WARNER

A BOOK, A SPOON, AND A FEW LITTLE MIRACLES

Published by Cardinal Rules Press

Cover art by Don W. Warner
Cover design by Patrick Burns
Edited and formatted by Marley Gibson
ISBN-13: 978-1533244178
ISBN-10: 1533244170

Cardinal Rules
PRESS

Endorsements

"I was transported back in time by this tense, yet tender memoir of a ten-year old girl whose family was deeply involved in the resistance during the Nazi occupation of the Netherlands. Ada's indomitable spirit and fierce Dutch pride in the face of German oppression lives on the pages and in your heart."

~ Kathleen Sandberg
Professor of English, Peking University, China

"After reading Ada's book about her childhood memories during the German occupation of her homeland, I was touched by the perspectives offered by this sweet young girl. Her family's sacrifice to be part of the resistance showed me the great love they had for their freedom, homeland, and their friends. Ada and her family lived through a very difficult time in the history of mankind, facing it with courage and love."

~ Bob Strong

"Ada Warner has gifted her readers with a gripping account of her experiences during Nazi occupied Holland. Told with both childlike innocence and the poignancy of a seasoned adult, she walks us through those dark, turbulent days. It would be easy to be weighed down by the urgency, the cruelties, and horrors of this frightful time, but this is not the case. Readers of all ages will be moved as their hearts soar with this inspiring story of courage, honor, and resolve."

~ Barbara Emanuelson
Author of MARIAH'S SONG

"Ada tells a heart breaking tale of suffering and hardships during WWII in an uplifting, even humorous, and heart-rendering way. Through this book, Ada's wish came true... for her stories to live on for her descendants and others to give an inside look into every day hardships during this time in history."

~ Drienie Hattingh
Author of FOREVER FRIENDS

"In this World War II memoir, Ada relates her childhood memories growing up in the Netherlands during the German's occupation. Always hungry, trying to keep warm, and trying to find a semblance of daily routine... her love of humanity shines through as her story unfolds."

~ Christy Monson
Award-winning author of BANISHED

Dedication

I dedicate these memories to our brother, Herman Overdiek, who in the "famous hungry winter" of 1944-1945, as it is now remembered in the Netherlands when he scoured the country sides looking for food for our family. We owe him for many a meal we ate because of his dedication to his family. Herman, at that time, was only seventeen-years-old and like any other young man his age, in the Netherlands, was at risk of being picked up by the enemy to work in the artillery factories in Germany. Herman is now ninety-years-old and still resides in Holland with his wife, Mienio, and two daughters, Janine and Francine.

In memory of our dearest Oma, who's diluted hot chocolate I can still taste while thinking about her. To our wildly impulsive Opa, who eventually did learn to stay away from open windows. And, to my siblings and our brave parents who so courageously fought the second World War in their own particular way along with many other patriots.

Acknowledgements

My thanks go to my good friend, Drienie Hattingh, a well-known author, for helping me with this project. I admire her talent and her latest publication, "Forever Friends," has found a special place in my home.

Thanks also to our fabulous seven! My children: Donnie, John, Susan, Karen, Jeff, Daren, and Christopher. They are my seven critics who never got tired listening to my stories through the years. Finally, my gratitude to our family's two computer geniuses, my daughters-in-law, Michelle and Renee, who were always ready at a moment's notice to help with anything to do with computers that were beyond me.

Therefore, fear not, little flock; do good; let earth and hell combine against you; for if ye are built upon my rock, they cannot prevail.

DOCTRINE AND COVENANTS 6:34

Ada and her mother, Betty.

Introduction

During the first days of early occupation of the Nazi regime in the Netherlands, decisions had to be made by the Dutch citizens.

"Are we going to do the best we can by tolerating this unwanted enemy or do we make a stand of defiance?"

The answer to this had been a simple one for my parents. *Resist!* This book is a recollection of events that faced the Overdiek family having engaged themselves in an underground resistance group against the occupying Nazi regime during the days of World War II.

These are stories documented from my experiences during the last years I lived in Holland between 1944 and 1945. I was ten years old at the time. Even at that tender age, when playing with dolls and marbles should have had been my priority, I instead became involved with my parents' underground endeavors. Through our difficult, challenging experiences, which our family and so many others faced, we trusted in a Higher Power and that goodwill would conquer the evil. In the end, this was a blessing.

It was only in 1993, a lifetime later, when I was living in America and recuperating from hip surgery, that I found the time to write these stories down after much encouragement from my family. These stories, after all, had entertained my children, my crew of seven, many times in the past. Perhaps families to come—our descendants—would find it interesting to read of these terrifying times in our beloved Holland and how we survived… together.

So, here is a glimpse into the past of our daily perils inflicted upon us by the Nazi regime…

Ten-year-old Ada during WWII.

Preface

It had been a peaceful existence, living in the western section of Amsterdam, close to the inner city of the lovely, century-old city—the capital of the Netherlands.

The neighborhood we lived in, for the most part, was a friendly one. The north part of our street ended on to a wide main road which bordered (De Nassau Kade) a large canal which in turn would flow into the Amstel canal.

Our home was located in the middle of a huge block of newly-built government housing. We lived on the main floor which gave us a quick access to the street. A single woman with her ailing old father lived just over us. Their dog, a German shepherd, was the delight of every child in the neighborhood.

A few apartment dwellings away, there lived an older gentleman whose birthday was the same as mine. He was all alone, so on June 2nd every year, Mr. Gravestein would surprise me with a birthday gift. He was a sweet old gentleman who dressed in the style of his generation, for my dear friend was a Jew. Our Jewish neighbor certainly dressed differently in comparison with our other neighbors. His traditional robe-style coat fitted loosely around his rather thin frame. A long braid of his hair poked out the back of a peculiar-looking black cap he'd wear. Also, I noticed that he always had several books under his arms as he would walk past our window.

Mother told me my Jewish benefactor was a professor. That also needed to be explained to me. Mother went on to say, "He is like the teachers in school. The only difference is," she continued, "he teaches his students about many important people in the Old Testament."

"Oh, yes, Mama. I know about them. They are called prophets, like Abraham."

The surprised look on mother's face told me she was happy I had paid attention to what had been taught to me in Sunday school.

Directly across from us lived a family who was originally from the eastern part of Europe, where they had immigrated from. Their daughter happened to be the same age as I was. She was a mean-spirited child, always ready to slap my face whenever something about me annoyed her. This kind of behavior could have been created because of the neighbor's lack of respect for the family. People often called them "the gypsies." Sadly enough, shortly after the war with Germany broke out, they suddenly disappeared.

At ten years old, I had two older brothers, Robert and Herman (whom we called Boy), from father's first marriage.

I also had three younger siblings, Johnny who was two years younger than me, followed my Martin, and then Nola, my baby sister, who was born in 1943.

Robert spent most of his time with his mother working in her deli shop, but Boy remained faithful to us and would go out into the country-side with a small handcart to look for food. He would go from one farm to another, but that's another story.

Since Father was very much involved with the Dutch underground resistance, we saw very little of him. Not only did he seem like a stranger to us because of his absence, he also seemed odd because of the Van Dyke beard he had grown to make his identification more difficult. See, Father and his colleagues were always dodging the Germans who seemed to be constantly nipping at their heels. It would have been difficult recognizing him even without the Van Dyke. His once full cheeks were now sunken in from the lack of nourishing food and giving his face a gaunt appearance. His otherwise clear blue eyes were often bloodshot from lack of sleep and changed their color to a dull grey.

Mother didn't look much better. Before the war, she often complained about how she would like to shed a few extra pounds. Little did she know this problem would be taken care of through no choice of her own. I remember Mother storing her share of bread in her apron pocket where she could nibble away at it through the day. It seemed like more food when she ate it that way, she claimed. It wasn't long before us kids found out about the stash in her apron. Our busy hands were often in her pockets searching for an extra piece of bread we were so hungry for. Mother wouldn't refuse her little ones which made her share smaller and smaller.

Her attitude stayed cheerful and happy most of the time, but with intervals of absentmindedness as if she were trying to block out all the pressures around her. Mother had a lovely trained voice. She would practice her beautiful music every morning, keeping the whole neighborhood entertained, providing it was summer and the windows were left open. She added a cheery note to our existence on Helmerstraat in Amsterdam.

Our next door neighbor lady of many years had become one of Mother's best friends. The neighbor's husband was drafted into the German army, much to his wife's dismay. He was the son of German refugees, making him draft material.

As strange as it may seem, our good fortune was she knew about Father's underground dealings. "If there's anything I can do, Betty," she told my mother. "I will be there for you."

This lady hated the Nazis with a passion. Her husband, a medic, was a good man. He had patched us kids up many times after a fall from the playground equipment or other such tomfoolery. Sure enough, she kept her faithful promise to my mother when our family desperately needed her help.

It so happened one time that Father had come home with a large bundle of illegal news bulletins that were printed on a monthly basis. Those bulletins were to be distributed between our regulars who picked up their share at our house, all done in a very organized way.

Nervertheless, on this particular day, the "regulars" had not picked them up as of yet. The neighbor's son came to our front door to warn Mother of a raid occuring on our street. Our neighbor asked if there was anything in our house that would bring harm to our family. Mother's face must have gone white when told of the raid. Even though it must have been very difficult to keep her generally calm composure, Mother told her about the bulletins.

"Betty," our neighbor said. "Get back in the house and throw those things over the fence... hurry, they are getting close!"

Mother did as she was told. Too bad she did not think to wrap them first for when she threw them over the fence, they went all over the neighbor's yard. Since our neighbor could prove her husband was in the German armed forces, the raiding soldiers left her home void from being searched.

The raid was luckily stopped by the time it was our turn.

The bulletins were quickly cleaned up.

Surely, we all were very blessed to have such a good neighbor.

It was fun growing up on our street. From our living room window, it was exciting to watch the rain fall on the pavement or to see the snow blanketing the sidewalk or listen to the thunder before the rain would fall, rumbling on and on for miles without mountains blocking the thunderous noises coming from the heavens above.

We enjoyed going to the neighborhood grocery store with our pennies to buy a jaw breaker or two or head around the corner, carrying Mother's lovely Delft blue milk can, to have the milkman fill it with a liter of *volle melk* (whole milk.)

Most certainly, I remembered waking up each Sunday morning with the sound of bells coming from the Westerkerk (Western Church) in our city, ringing in our ears. Then, there was the Sunday morning breakfast before we would go to church, consisting of soft-boiled eggs, a drink of buttermilk, and Mother's fluffy pancakes.

All these peaceful reminders were there to be appreciated by all in our part of the world.

Then, in the beginning of May 1940, early one morning, all our peaceful existence was interrupted by a very noisy radio announcing we were at war with Germany…

"Heil Hitler" was repeated constantly throughout the broadcast. The harsh voices coming from the radio spoken in a foreign tongue would have frightened the devil himself. Us children huddled around, too scared to speak a word. Mother's tears never stopped coming, especially when we watched out the window of our house as the German soldiers marched through our streets singing their military songs.

Suddenly, the familiar and safe surrounding of our home became an unfamiliar place. The very gates of Hell seemed to have opened up and manifested itself in our homes and country.

Memories of this devastating newscast bring me back to a tearful mother and four very frightened children. When Father heard the news of the invasion, he hurried home from his office.

After counseling his tearful family, he said, "It is going to be a rough road ahead, *lieverd* (sweet one)."

Mother dried her tears and replied, "Give me a bowl, a spoon, and a few little miracles and I will help keep the home fires burning."

The place in Holland where Dutch people stood in line for soup during WWII.

Chapter One

OUR LITTLE CORNER

The struggle for existence in our war-torn country became more challenging as time went on. Mother made her food ration coupons for bread, potatoes, and vegetables last as long as possible by serving small portions of food. For breakfast, one slice of bread, and for dinner, a small potato, and another slice of bread. Lunch time had been eliminated a long time past.

She complained bitterly one day after standing in line for a long period of time to anyone who would be willing to hear how unfair it was that the food rations were cut down again. The woman at the office building handing out the coupons after proper ID had been shown, whispered to Mother to be careful. Mother nodded in agreement. To her dismay, the small ration of butter issued in the past for young children under the age of three had also been cancelled.

When Mother got home, telling us all about her day, she calmed down, but not after Father had warned her not to express her opinion in public about the unfairness of war.

Through all of this, Mother tried to stay cheerful. She'd often gather us around the old antique organ Father had surprised her with and sing our favorite song about a puppy who was cute to behold, but became very annoying as an adult dog with his barking. This cute little nursery song had, on many occasions in the past, calmed the fears of her four children.

Father had no choice but to equally divide his time between our family and his dedication to the underground.

"We can't fight them with guns, but we can make their lives a little more complicated. We can help others with shelter, food, and information," Father stated.

Food had become increasingly scarce; even the black market dealer had very little to offer their eager customers. The only rationed items left were potatoes and some root vegetables like carrots, turnips, and sugar beets. All other coupons were cancelled with the exception of bread coupons. The portions received for a person was barely enough food to sustain life.

There were many complaints, but for the most part, the Dutch citizens bore their burdens well. The Dutch always were a stubborn lot, reluctant to give up in spite of many difficult circumstances they had been confronted with, whether past or present.

Occupation by an unwanted enemy dated as far back as the days of the Roman Empire when the lowlands became one of the many conquered countries in Europe, captured by the fast-growing empire of the Romans. Even the great emperor, Napoleon Bonaparte, wouldn't allow this tiny country to slip by unnoticed while planning his aggressive war ambitions to attain Europe. In the outcome, the courageous people of Holland finally did succumb to the aggressor, the Emperor Napoleon.

Soon after the take-over, the Emperor crowned his brother, Louis, as Holland's new king. In spite of hostile feelings for this hated enemy on their throne, the new king, in time, became a loved and respected monarch who contributed much toward furthering education for the masses. He also supported the cultures of Holland, taking to his credit the construction of many lovely theaters where the Dutch citizens were able to enjoy the artistic refinement of the popular composers of that era.

Decades later, our so-loved country once more became the focus of another aggressor from a neighboring country. Once again, our hardy breed of people faced the difficulties of war. Indeed, it would be out of character for them to refuse to look on the bright side of their situation. At the moment, however, only the negative seemed to be nipping away at this positive attitude the Dutch had so dedicated themselves to. Surely, their empty bellies being the severest of all tests of bravery didn't inspire maintaining a positive attitude. Nevertheless, sustained with a love of God and country, strengthened with a strong desire for independence and freedom, the Dutch kept their spirits like a blazing fire burning in their very souls, continually fanned by the courage the war forced upon them.

Mother had more than her hands full trying to feed her family. In addition to her problems, Father's parents had become an extra responsibility. Their wellbeing was a constant source of worry because the war had left its telltale signs with these two dear people. The lack of good and nutritious food had them in a weakened state.

Perhaps with the newly-installed soup kitchens in different parts of each neighborhood, some extra portions could be shared with the grandparents. The kitchen which supplied our neighborhood was an old elementary school located half a city block from our home. Cleverly enough, that bit of extra food for them was obtained with the falsified ration cards supplied by the underground resistance group.

At the time, my parents felt I was responsible enough to take my turn in the food line. Nevertheless, it was a scary experience standing in the long line waiting my turn for a meager ration of watery soup, yet knowing the card held in my hand had been falsified. When I complained about how the guards, with their big guns strapped on their back, frightened me, my older brother, Herman, took over. Mother would stand in the line for the first shift followed by Herman for the second shift. It was done in this manner so as not to arouse suspicion for the total number of family members indicated on the ration cards. If it had been discovered that more than one member of the family stood in one line, each having a card, we certainly would have been questioned by the guards and this could have led to imprisonment.

Luckily, we were never found out.

It was a good mile and a half walk to our grandparents' home from our house. My job was to bring Opa (grandpa) and Oma (grandma) the soup so skillfully obtained with the extra ration cards. This had become my permanent responsibility since Herman took over my place in the soup line.

In better days, the walking distance between our home and our grandparents' had been an entertaining one, for the street they lived on once used to be an open market place. It spanned at least two blocks and was divided by two streets running through both market areas, hence dividing the markets into two parts. The location of the fish market was easily identified by the overwhelming odors coming from the south side of the market. However, the more sophisticated wares which were offered on the opposite side of the market were, by far, the more colorful and exciting.

My grandparents lived in a grand, old apartment dwelling on the first floor located in the center of the two block area of the market. The large windows of their apartment opened up to the panorama below, providing them with almost around-the-clock entertainment. Sadly enough, for some time, the main characters of this colorful gigantic stage that once existed below their windows—the vendors and their bargain-hunting customers—had long since disappeared from the scene for the lack of wares.

The deprivation of our small country by the Nazis was noticeable everywhere and was suffered by almost everyone. On entering this empty street, which once buzzed with excitement, I longed for the old way of life.

I could feel a melancholy spirit for what once was, lingering endlessly in these lonely memories. A few skeletons of unclaimed vendor carts were carelessly abandoned after having been robbed of most of their available substance. They stood in shambles on their sides. When listening closely, the beckoning call of the owners could still be heard, "Strawberries, strawberries, come and get yours now."

Afraid to move, as if not to break the spell, I was totally caught up in the now imaginary world of what once existed here, not long ago.

"Ribbons, ribbons, pretty ribbons for your hair. Here, here! Look at those colors, *kom kyken*, come look, come!"

Full of convincing charm, these peddlers could tempt even the most reluctant of browsers.

My thoughts traveled farther up the street to where, proudly flying the red, white, and blue Dutch flag, once stood the most colorful herring stand in the old capital of Holland. Eager people wanting to buy the first catch of the season would gather round the tiny herring stands. As tradition would have it, the first herring was to be presented to the Queen of the Netherlands.

Mother seldom missed her Wednesday afternoon market days to shop for fresh vegetables. Somehow or another, she always had a nickel to spare for a sour pickle, which were sold from one of the two huge wooden barrels standing on opposite ends of the herring stand.

"Here, help yourself," the proprietor would say, handing one a spear-like fork with a long handle after I gave him my money. Bobbing for the biggest pickle in the barrel generally took some doing. After the first wonderful bite, that squirted pickle juice in all directions, I felt it had been worth the effort.

For a few magical moments, the past had become part of reality.

Out of the blue I heard, "Watch out!" The abrupt words of an irritated boy trying to avoid from hitting me with his bike, sounded harsh in the quiet afternoon.

I quickly jumped backward out of his way, up onto the sidewalk from where I had strayed while daydreaming. Gone were the wonderful sounds of the bygone yesterdays, wiped away by a stranger on a bike.

My sudden jerk had spilled the soup, soiling the towel the pan had been wrapped in. "Oh, how rude he was. Look at this!" It was my turn to be annoyed. This wouldn't go unnoticed, and I would surely be in trouble. "But, never mind," I said and giggled with confidence. "Oma loves me too much to allow herself to be angry with me."

Thoughts of her prompted me to look up at her apartment. As if by magic, she appeared at the window, smiling down on her favorite granddaughter. *How wonderfully old-fashioned she looks in her high-collared dress,* I thought fondly.

She stood tall, looking very lovely in the light of the setting sun. Her dark hair, now laced with silver, was softly pulled back and then twisted in a bun, worn on the back of her head. The escape of an occasional curly lock of hair, unwilling to stay put, gave her a soft look of elegance. Just then, the light of the afternoon sun caught the brilliance of her diamond broach

"Oh," I said with a gasp. "It looks like a beautiful star."

After returning my greeting, Oma hurried away from the window. At any moment, I'd expected to hear the click of the door opening. It was followed with a cheerful invite, "*Kom boven,*" come on up.

The steps going up were steep and narrow; therefore, I climbed them very carefully. I would spread my legs slightly to have more balance as I trotted up. It felt much like being a duck out of water, stumbling up the steps, in such a ridiculous manner. However, I dared not risk spilling more of the soup. The stairs ended in a dark hall which I preferred to ignore. A turn to the left led to the entrance door of the living quarters, opening up into a spacious entrance hall.

"Well, my dear girl, what have you brought me this time?"

No doubt she had been watching my struggle up the steps, for she could hardly speak from laughing so hard.

"Oma!" I complained.

"Oh, dear, I'm so sorry, but you looked so funny coming up the stairs like that."

Taking the full advantage of the situation, I found this a very good time to tell her about the spilled soup.

"Oh, never mind," she answered casually, still giggling while taking the pan from me.

After receiving a soft kiss on the cheek, she invited me to follow her into the kitchen.

"Opa, wake up! Come look what our granddaughter has brought us," she said, repeating it one more time in the direction of the bedroom, only this time with a voice full of irritation. "He sleeps too much," she grumbled while setting the pan down on her coal stove. "I'll rinse the towel clean and you will take it next time?"

"Oh, um, sure," I replied, very happy to have been relieved of the burden of spilled soup. I relaxed on one of her spotlessly clean white-painted chairs.

Oma's kitchen was small, which was typical of a big city dwelling. Empty wall space had been utilized with colorful painted shelves decorated with her own crocheted shelf edgings and displaying her priceless Delft blue plate collection. It added much warmth to the charm of the kitchen.

"Are you comfortable?" she asked. "As soon as your grandfather comes out of the bedroom, I'll make the three of us some hot cocoa."

"C-c-cocoa," I stammered in total surprise. "Where ever did you get cocoa?"

She laughed at my surprised reaction, "Never you mind, young lady, but we have to mix it with water."

"It will be wonderful, Oma. Besides, I prefer it with water," I lied.

"I know what to do," she said quietly. "I'll sweeten it with a bit of honey. Would you like that?"

"Yes, that would be nice."

I was surprised she had honey in the cupboard as well. She must love me dearly, I thought, to share something as precious as honey with me.

She continued, "We'll wake up your opa and then we'll have a party, just the three of us. Remember our parties, *lieverd,* before..." she paused. "Before well... you know."

"I know," I whispered.

Poor Oma, she hated the very mention of the word, *war.* She had barely been able to erase the memory of losing a much-loved cousin in the last one. Occasionally, when the subject was brought up in conversation between family members, she would often compare one with the other.

"This problem is by far the worst of the two. I can't remember having been this hungry before." Afraid to complain and almost too embarrassed to go on, she would whisper, "Even in the worst of times, there was always something to eat."

The smell of the cocoa powder as it mixed with hot water in her lovely bone china tea cups interrupted my thoughts. The wonderful aroma of chocolate filled her kitchen as the water bubbled its way to the rim of the cups. In the few moments it took to fill the teacups, I felt the same sadness when entering the long, lonely street below us.

This is how life should be lived, I thought. *Warm and secure with family together enjoying a wonderful treat.*

"Penny for your thoughts," said Oma.

I did not reply.

"Two pennies for your thoughts? Come on, no secrets," she teased.

"No secrets, Oma. We need to be happy, huh?"

"Of course, *lieverd*. We are." She threw me one of her mischievous smiles, managing to put me in a better frame of mind. "Oh, how we love our parties," she mused as she placed the delicate cup and saucer filled with its precious brew on the table in front of her.

"Uh hum," I nodded in agreement, remembering her special parties meant only to entertain her grandchildren. Many wonderful treats were enjoyed around this very table. Apple cakes, cookies, and wonderful, thick buttermilk sweetened with a teaspoon of sugar "to wash the treats down with," she would say.

On many occasions, Oma would go shopping on the south side of the market for her favorite items. The vendors knew her well. They made sure only the freshest and biggest shrimp would find their way into her large cooking pot. In turn, my grandparents were anxious to share their feast with me, which I, without the slightest hesitation, politely refused. The memory of those poor critters making their frantic sounds and trying to escape their hot boiling fate nearly broke my heart.

"Oma?"

She turned slightly in my direction.

"Do you miss your shrimp parties?'

Her reaction was unexpected. She abruptly put the silver spoon down that she'd been stirring the cocoa with and gave me a stare so full of melancholy that I instantly regretted having asked her the question.

"I'm sorry, so sorry. I shouldn't have asked," I said, trying to correct my insensitive question.

"Oh," she responded, all of a sudden cheerful again. "I'll bet you don't miss them a-tinker's-darn, do you?" She burst into a happy laugh.

I eagerly followed, grateful she still knew how to laugh under these harsh circumstances we all lived under.

She got up slowly from the table, suddenly looking weary. "I'll go get Opa. His cocoa is getting cold."

I mustn't stay long, I thought.

Oma's dress hung loose around her slight frame, a dead giveaway that a few good meals would do her wonders. I watched her disappear into the sitting room. She had been a lovely woman in her younger years. Traces of beauty, now faded, were still noticeable in her much older, appearance.

Opa had always been proud of his attractive wife, forever showing his affection and appreciation in many ways. His reputation of having been one of the most skilled diamond cutters in the Amsterdam diamond factory had earned this grand old gentleman a good income, providing his family with a comfortable lifestyle. Oma's thriftiness, however, wouldn't allow him to live the more elegant lifestyle he would have preferred for his wife and children.

The many exquisite jewelry pieces created by her admiring husband, just for her, had been carefully locked away in a black ebony jewelry box. That was all, except one rather large diamond broach. Oma knew her husband was proud of this particular piece he had designed for her, so she wore it faithfully.

To her dismay, Opa had many moments of frequent generosity. It wouldn't be at all unusual for him to buy all the contents of a vendor's cart full of imported oranges from sunny Spain. Then, on the top of his lungs he'd shout, "Come and get it, kids!" Children in the market place adored him. He truly was the Pied Piper.

At one time, our unpredictable grandpa went too far testing his wife's patience. This incident had become the talk of the neighborhood. Perhaps this story had even reached beyond the boundaries of the neighborhood. It has become one of everyone's favorite stories, not only our family, to tell.

For some time, Oma had wanted to replace Grandpa's much-loved rocker for a new one. Over time, the rocker had become an extremely sore subject between the two of them. One day, dear Opa came home early from work. He walked right past his surprised wife, into the sitting room, and without saying a word, he opened both windows. Oma looked on, too dumbfounded to say anything.

Then, he walked back into the front room where he picked up his rocking chair. To Oma's total amazement, he returned to the sitting room, carrying the rocking chair, and, giving people on the street below proper warning, he tossed it out onto the street below, right before Oma's horror-stricken eyes.

"That wasn't the end of it," she shrieked when relating the story. "He went back into the room to pick up whatever furniture he could lift and tossed it out after the rocker."

When it was all done, he straightened his clothes, fixed his tie, turned toward his outraged wife, and said in a very calm voice, "See what nagging will get you?"

Luckily for Opa, the new furniture he'd ordered was on its way down the street on a horse-drawn wagon to be delivered moments after this much-talked about stunt. There was no doubt about it—he had a way of keeping life interesting for Oma.

"Opa, come out of there and say hello to your granddaughter," she said with her voice holding some irritation of before. "Your drink is getting cold, dear."

A slight groan coming from the direction of his room indicated that he got out of his new rocker and was on his way in.

"Pick up your feet, Opa, or Oma will call you lead foot," I called out.

She looked over at me grinning. "Oh, well," she sighed. "Will he ever learn?"

Squinting against the brightness of the room, Opa stumbled over to the window to draw the drapes shut. His general appearance had changed from impeccable to borderline sloppy. It was difficult for me to see them struggle and trying to survive their hardships.

"Hello, child," he barely whispered his greeting.

"Sit, sit," Oma ordered him. "Look what she brought us. Look, Pa."

"Yes, yes, I see," he grumbled in a sleepy voice. He expressed his gratitude with a smile directed at me. After a quick sip of his cocoa, sleepiness seemed to have left him. With a concerned look on his face, he commented, "I don't want to scare you, child, but remember there may be a person out there in greater need of that pan of soup who is willing to take it away from you. Next time, put it in a shopping bag. It can be done without spilling if done carefully."

"Yes, yes," Oma joined in. "Because you could get hurt."

"Oh," I said, suddenly quite frightened. "Would they really…?"

"Hurt you?" she said, completing my sentence.

Before I could go on, Oma got up from her chair to pull me toward her. She didn't say a word for a moment or so, but just stood there holding me. Then, in a voice barely above a whisper, she said, "Oh, how I wish that every scared and hungry soul out there could be held in a pair of loving arms, protecting them from all evil existing in so many places." She shivered with emotion.

I stayed very still, feeling her sadness pierce through me and causing a strange feeling of concern I didn't understand. It was her fear she had expressed as only a mother could feel. Dread for her loved ones, anxiety for the innocent somewhere out there who were at the mercy of "The Great Demon of War." Still overwhelmed with emotion, she steered me to the chair where I had carelessly thrown my coat.

Greatly affected by his wife's downhearted spirit, Opa rushed by her side. "Mama, let me. I'll help the child with her coat. You sit down. Please sit down, dear." His manner was tender, a part of him seldom revealed.

I felt the lump in my throat, my chest heavy with sorrow for these so-loved people. He helped her get into her chair. Her face appeared angelic, while she gazed up at him with a somewhat embarrassed smile of gratitude.

Poor Oma, I thought sadly. *She's a far cry from the spunky person of a moment ago.*

"Are you warm enough?" he asked while tucking a blanket around her waist and legs. "I'll put some wood in the stove; we'll have a cozy fire in a moment. Would you like that?"

Oma's hand shook as she touched his arm in a form of an answer.

He continued talking to her in the same comforting manner. "We'll talk about when the children were young while the fire in the stove is warming up. You'll like that, won't you dear?"

"Oh, yes," she replied with her voice weary and drained of all strength. She added, "That would be nice."

With a familiar groan, he straightened himself out of the stooped position he had been in while consoling her. He shuffled his way into the kitchen, searching for the matches he couldn't find.

Here was my chance to help. I knew the matches always had a prominent place on the top of the coal stove shelf. "Here, here they are, they're here!"

He chuckled while taking them from me. Sheepishly, he said, "I knew that."

Ordinarily, I wouldn't have missed a chance to have teased him about that remark, but right now wasn't the time to do so. "I'll get some wood for the fire, okay, Opa?"

"Yes, child. Thank you. Do you know where it is stacked?"

"If it's still in the hall, under the stairs, I do."

A grumpy sort of noise came from his direction.

Supposing it meant "yes," I made my way to the wood closet, but not without a bit of hesitation, for the hall was dark and daunting. My imagination had more than once gotten the best of me, prompting me to believe evil monsters, so hideous, were ready to jump out at me. I would even make the bravest person whimper with deathly fright.

Oh, how silly! I thought boldly, *that kind of nonsense is kid stuff.*

"Opa, may I leave the door open while I fetch the wood?" I asked partly losing my courage.

However, Opa came to the rescue with a hand worked flashlight. Nerve lost a few moments ago, restored itself with him my by side. "Just turn the doorknob, child. It opens quite easily."

The door swung in exposing a huge amount of chopped firewood. "Oh, Opa," I said with a gasp. "You should keep this door locked."

"No need for that. If someone steals wood, child, it wouldn't be because of greed, but because they are cold like most everyone. Therefore, they are welcome to it."

Too young to understand his most incredible generosity, I urged him once more to lock the closet just the same.

The light went dim from the flashlight. "Hurry, child. My hand is nearly worn out pumping this worthless thing."

Loading my arms with as much wood as I could carry, we quickly left this dreaded dark hall to move into friendlier surroundings.

Oma sat silent, seemingly unaware of the great effort of Opa starting a fire in the stove. It wasn't long before the crackling sound of burning wood filled the room with a cozy comfort.

It was time for me to leave. Opa had the situation well in hand.

"Good-bye, Oma, Opa..." I said softly.

"Thank you, child, for your visit. Please thank your parents also and give them our love."

"Oh, Opa." I nearly swept him off his feet with a most sincere-felt hug.

"I know," he said with a weary sigh. "We'll be all right. Go now, before it turns dark out."

He allowed me to hold onto him for a few moments longer. His woolen sweater smelled faintly of sweet pipe tobacco, it being so much a part of him, and felt soft and warm against my face.

I left quickly, but not without hesitation.

Depiction of Ada and her cat, Hummus, having to find a safe place to hide when the bombs dropped from the sky. Sketch by Ada's husband, Don.

Chapter Two

THE KITTEN

A gush of cold evening air blew against my face upon entering the market place. A chill ran through me as I dreaded the walk home. Huge clouds in the form of enormous beasts of prey crowding their way forward, created a foreboding danger. My steps quickened, as I longed to be home with my family whom, at this moment, seemed to be a thousand light years away. Fright fell over me, a feeling I was well familiar with. I kept walking, spurring myself on with every step I'd take. The streets were almost totally deserted by now. Few people were to be seen anywhere near.

A feeling of doom seemed to have engulfed the streets. I shivered underneath my coat more from anxiety than the evening cold. The empty display windows of the neighborhood shops resembled dark gaping holes much like Oma's dark hall, hiding hideous creatures ready to jump out at their unsuspecting victims.

Fright turned into panic.

Ultimately finding safety in the middle of the road, away from the dreadfully gaping dark window, I started to run. The cold air hurt my chest with every breath I'd take.

Soon now, the bridge over the canal would come into view. Visions of the familiar landmark spurred me on.

Several people on their bikes raced by, not having interest in me nor taking the time to notice anything, being only conscious of their own troubled predicament. Their bended bodies toiled hard against the harsh, unforgiving wind. It took all the strength they had to keep their bikes from straying off the road.

I raised my arm in a gesture for help, but they disappeared over the bridge. That same lonely, urgent feeling swept over me once again, like a heavy black shroud. I could feel splashes of raindrops attacking my face, almost warm against my cold skin. *Good,* I thought, *the rain will calm this brutal wind.*

Suddenly, there came the severe clattering noise of a garbage can tipping over from the powerful wind. It fell hard against the cement, then caught by the gale, it kept rolling down the street. A high-pitched screech followed the clatter of the rolling trash can.

Before I knew it, a skinny, little, black and white cat, who had been scrounging for food, darted right in front of me. Holding his thick bushy tail straight up in the air, he scampered as fast as he could across the street. I stood watching, too surprised to move a muscle.

Luckily for him, there was no one else around or he would have been someone's dinner tonight. *Poor thing, He's forever doomed,* I thought sadly. *I could fetch him, but no, I need to go home—I must go home.*

My legs seemed to have frozen on the spot. A decision had to be made. Do I save this poor stray or do I leave it to fend for itself?

There was no need for discussion. Swiftly, the penetrating sound of the alarm sirens filled the air with its deafening sound. Oh, how they screeched. I held my hand over my ears, trying to muffle the noise.

I tried to remember what Mother had taught me to do in case of an air raid which this certainly was. Too terrified to remember, I looked around for help. Some distance away, people were running only to disappear in surrounding homes.

Tears of frustration filled my eyes. I knew time was essential. I had to find shelter to protect myself from possible falling fragments. Thumping with tremendous beats, my heart seemed as though it had moved from my chest to my throat.

"Where do I go? Hide! Hide!" I could hardly breathe.

Then, in the worst part of this dreadfully panicky moment, I remembered one of those special instants between my parents and their children when concern for them was extreme.

"My children, the time may come when we encounter a hopeless situation," Papa had said. "No matter what it is, when there does not seem to be much hope for a solution, remember, there is someone who cares for you very much. This someone will always be there when called upon."

This sounded very much like grown up talk to me, but I knew my father meant our Heavenly Father, a higher power, would protect me.

My heart seemingly quit thumping, but best of all, the sirens had stopped their howling noise. The gift of comfort and assurance, through prayer, had not been ignored because of the panic within me.

All at once I knew what to do...

The two metal bins the cat had scampered off to! Yes, that was where I would go.

Still shaken and unsteady, my hand automatically went to my eyes, wiping the tears away. "Off you go now, hurry," I told myself.

I knew the roar of the airplane engines would soon replace the silence of the sirens. A wonderful feeling of determination replaced the dread I felt just minutes before. The strength needed to make good, sound decisions was the reward of my prayer said.

It took seconds before the distance between me and the bins disappeared. I crouched down behind the dumpster located farthest from the street. The overhanging from the building next to the dumpster provided me with shelter from the drizzling rain. Dozens of cardboard boxes flattened and bundled in large squares were stacked along the back of the wall untouched by the weather. It took all of my strength to drag them to the side of the dumpster. Once that was accomplished, I started picking away at the rope holding them together.

The ground was cold and damp and penetrated through my clothes. The rope scraped roughly against my icy hands. Pressure from the weight of the boxes had in time tightened the knot. In spite of the burning pain caused by the roughness of the rope, I kept picking away at it, when finally it gave way to my prying fingers. For only a tiny moment, I felt bad that I had taken advantage of someone's effort by destroying their work.

I placed several of the flattened boxes underneath me, quickly losing any sense of guilt while enjoying the comfort the boxes provided from the damp ground underneath. Soon, that empty feeling of loneliness was present all over again with the only sound to be heard was that of the falling rain splashing on the scattered boxes surrounding me. Tension held me in its iron grip convincing me the worst was yet to come. I cuddled up against the wall seeking some form of comfort against the cold, hard brick.

"Why didn't I run faster? I could have been home by now. Why didn't I leave Oma's house immediately when she wanted me to?" I asked out loud to no one while feelings of reproach and regrets pounded away at me.

No, I thought firmly. *Think of good things.*

I tried visualizing Oma sitting by the fire with Opa making a fuss over her.

In the far distance, the roaring sound of airplanes approaching could be heard. The gray skies of just moments before were being threatened by the conquest of war.

A terrified screech escaped me.

Numb with fear and cold, I cuddled even closer to the wall. "Oh, Oma!" I sobbed. "I don't want to be here. If only I could be with you."

I placed my hands over my ears, trying to muffle the sounds of the planes of the Allies coming closer. "It was never this scary before. Why is it so scary now?" I asked as I moaned.

Hysterically, I screamed out answering my own question. "You'd be in your warm bed then all snug and safe."

The planes were almost right above me, filling the sky with their terrifying sounds.

"No, no," I said through my tears. "I don't want to hear this. *Stop!* I want it to stop." My body shook with violent sobs. I had never felt so alone. Then, in the midst of my despair, something soft and warm nudged at my arm, followed by a loud purring noise.

My heart soared when I realized what so desperately wanted my attention. A wonderful thing was happening. I had been sent a little companion to see me through this very bad ordeal. And, she had been sent to me, as well. No one could ever understand what I experienced when I reached out to hold the same shaggy, skinny cat I had seen earlier.

The horrifying reverberations and booms coming from above me were instantly forgotten. Though frightened, the cat stayed very still in my arms. Her whiskers tickled my nose and she licked my tear-stained face. I could feel her heart beat rapidly against my hand while holding her.

"Here now, little girl," I whispered holding my face close to her tiny body. "I am so glad you have come to share my corner with me."

She peered up at me with a certain understanding. Her eyes were big and hollow, brought on by hunger and suffering. Still purring, she snuggled in my arms, resting herself as if she had forever belonged there.

"Poor little thing. You must have been on the run for a long time and from the looks of you, I know you are as brave as your cousin, the great lion."

This absurd comparison made me laugh in spite of myself as I glanced down at this dirty, skinny, diminutive creature, now snuggling against me and purring in comfort. Then, unexpectedly, with her whiskers spread apart very wide, she woke up with a start, pushing her wet face in the direction of my coat pocket. She let out a slight noise, resembling a polite "meow" backed up with a rather firm nudge against that same pocket. This reminded me of the emergency cracker stashed there.

"Oh, dear, little one!" I cried out. "You must be starved. Here, here, for it is yours."

Her body grew tense with excitement while watching me take the cracker out of my pocked. She watched every move I made as I broke the cracker in several pieces and softened it with rain water dripping from the overhang. The smell of the food nearly left her frantic.

"Easy, little one, easy now."

She choked down the food in huge gulps resulting with her body reacting as in a state of convulsion.

"Poor little one, it has been a long time between meals, hasn't it?"

Anxious for more, her large, hollow eyes looked up at me, but I could only give her an apology for not having more food to offer her. She nudged me in gentle understanding. With her tummy filled somewhat, she had grown less tense. I watched her with delight while she turned her body several times in my lap before she made herself comfortable. Almost instantly, she fell fast asleep, purring her melody of contentment.

I felt an abiding love for this kitten, so often called by many a worthless creature. Her problems had ended with a water-soaked cracker.

At last, she belonged.

A typical Dutch home.

Chapter Three

AGATHA'S BOYFRIEND

The tranquil scene in our corner was suddenly disturbed by a sharp explosion.

Huge beams of searchlights coming from below like giant snakes were now probing the black skies above. They were all too successful in finding their unfortunate targets. Once again, an Allied plane had fallen prey to the enemy below. The aircraft exploded in horror as gravity sucked it into its waiting arms.

The chase was on. Totally ignoring that the 'all clear siren' had not been given, I started running, clutching the little cat in my arm, against my chest. Again, thoughts of home where we'd be safe prodded me on and on until I had finally reached one of the many old flower stands by the bridge close to home. Needing a moment of rest, I leaned wearily against the railing. It had stopped raining. The air smelled fresh and clean with the earthly smell I so loved. All at once, the turmoil above had stopped as quickly as it had started. A sigh of relief escaped my dry throat. Surprisingly, the tiny creature tucked away under my coat never stopped purring through everything. My thought turned toward home once again.

"I guess I won't be surprised if I have to do dishes for a week," I murmured, knowing I should have left Oma's much sooner.

As we got close to home, my steps changed from frisky to very slow. Somewhat reluctantly, I turned the last corner entering my street not knowing what to expect—a tongue lashing, a week of dishwashing duty, or maybe a spanking. Then, with the last grain of courage left in me after the harrowing experience, I turned the corner.

It nearly took my breath away when I noticed the front door of our home stood wide open. Just then, my little brother, Johnny, came peeking out of the doorway looking up and down the street as though he was expecting someone. In spite of his young age, the nine-year-old was as tough and street wise as any kid twice his age. I couldn't help chuckling once again remembering how I'd caught him crying when Mother read him the Cinderella story. He's a tough kid with a kind heart. He also had been well-indoctrinated keeping our parents' underground activities a guarded secret.

"Johnny, what's wrong? What are you doing out here?"

When he turned my way; I could see the stress on his young face. He hurried over to me, grabbed my hand, and pulled me toward the front door of the house. He didn't speak. Once in the house, he whispered, "Sis, there is a soldier in our front room."

My grip tightened on his hand, turning him around, so I could look him square in the face and then asked rather forcefully, "Johnny, what are you saying?"

"Yes, honest. Agatha brought him with her. She wants Papa to hide him!"

"Hide him? What do you mean, hide him? Wait! Is he a German soldier?"

"Well, yes. What else?" was his impatient answer. Now, near to tears, he continued, "He's awfully tall and he's Agatha's boyfriend."

We both stood there together for a few moments in stunned silence. The quiet was broken when, still in an unbelieving frame of mind, I asked, "Agatha, our cousin?"

Johnny nodded his head. "You don't believe me?"

"I believe you, I do."

Oh, how we both wished it wasn't what it appeared to be. It was hard to imagine our beautiful cousin, Agatha, would betray her country by fraternizing with a German soldier, the enemy. By now, Johnny was pulling me toward the open front door.

"Get away from there, Johnny," I urged him. "We need to close the door. What are you looking for?"

"We can't close the door, Sis. I need to see if he's coming."

Johnny's behavior started to worry me. "Who's coming?"

"Hitler," he said nervously, glancing over his shoulder.

"Hitler? Why Hitler" I asked. I was totally convinced at that moment that my brother had gone mad.

"Yes, he's looking for Agatha's boyfriend."

"Oh, get in here and shut the door," I said impatiently. "Hitler is not going to bother us."

After a few explanations, I managed to convince Johnny that Hitler was too busy to get involved.

The hushed voices, which came from the front room, were suddenly replaced with loud angry words.

"See," Johnny whispered nervously, holding back tears. Forgotten were the air raid and my new cat who, by now, had found it necessary to explore her new surroundings. She discovered a place to relax behind the coat rack after she escaped from the security of my arms. The shocked look on Johnny's face momentarily made me once again forget about the situation facing all of us.

His eyes widened when he asked, "Can I have her?"

There was no time to answer him for just then the front room door opened. It was Mother. Her face, generally pale from the lack of proper nourishment, was now flushed with nervous anxiety. Her first question directed at me was, "Where have you been?"

"Mama, I'm sorry. I stayed too long at Oma's. I did try to hurry, though."

"Never mind now," she said distractedly. "We will discuss this later."

The voices coming from the front room grew more intense. Mother wrung her hands in frustration, when finally she spotted my new companion. "A cat?" she exclaimed.

"Please, Mama, let us keep her. Johnny and I will take care of her."

The answer to that question wasn't needed for Mother was a great cat lover. We could tell her heart was already softened. "We'll discuss this later, as well, but right now I want you both to be good kids and get yourselves ready for bed."

This was not the right time to ask a lot of questions, but there was one needing an explanation. "Mama, is there a German soldier in the front room with Papa and Agatha?"

Before answering, she pulled both of us in the far corner of the foyer. "Yes," she whispered, urging us to never tell anyone what had occurred tonight.

"We know, Mama. Don't worry," I whispered, while Johnny nodded with his eyes big.

She smiled approvingly, knowing she could count on us.

"Why is he here in our home? He's a *German* soldier," I said.

She leaned against the wall burying her face in her hands. A sob escaped from her.

Johnny managed to give me a good kick and said accusingly, "Look what you did."

"No, no. I'm fine kids. Agatha," she whispered while keeping her eyes on the front room door, "wants to marry this soldier. She has brought him here for Father to hide him away."

"We can hide him under the bed," Johnny suggested, which made Mama smile.

She went on to say, "This man has done some bad thing and the police want to put him in jail. Now, no more questions. Go to bed. Marty is asleep and so is Nola. Be very quiet not to wake them."

The angry voices in the front room had quieted down and were replaced with soft sobs.

Sleep came, but not instantly. The little cat snuggled with Johnny in his bed.

"What are we going to name her?" Johnny asked.

"I thought about Hummus," I replied.

"Hummus? That's a weird name, Sis."

"Well, that's what it's going to be because I found her."

"Okay, I like it. Hey, where did you find her anyway?"

"I don't want you to know, all right?" I snapped at him.

"Geez, you are mean. I don't want to know anyway." His sleepy voice trailed off into a whisper, "Goodnight, Sissy."

Angrily, I turned my back on him. "You know I hate it when you call me Sissy."

"Umm, yeah, I'm sorry."

Well, I knew he was not. "One more thing, if you ever call me that again, I'm going to tell Mama and Papa how you took those wooden blocks from between the train tracks and that the Germans shot at you and the others while you were stealing them. Yeah, that will get you into trouble good."

The threat took no effect on him. Instead, he sat himself straight up in bed and boasted, "Yes, I stole those stupid blocks, but we had a cooked dinner that night, didn't we, Sissy?"

I thought that deserved a good old poke.

"Hey! What is it now?" he complained.

"Did you say your prayers?" I asked, still mad at him.

"I can't say them without Mama here."

"Yes, you can. Just say them the way Sister Hilda in primary taught us."

"If I do, will you then be still?" he asked.

"Yes, okay."

He lay back down, pulled his covers over his head, and mumbled his prayers.

In spite of my accusations to him, I was very proud of what he had done, stealing those wooden blocks.

Punishment for stealing could be severe. On rare occasions, those stealing blocks were shot at by the Nazis who happened to be controlling the neighborhood. Hunger and cold can override common sense. Little John managed to carry a block home with him even though it weighed a good ten pounds.

"A nice man gave me one," he'd said.

We couldn't ask for a braver and more determined brother for it was indeed brave of this spunky nine-year-old to participate with the grown-ups stealing wooden blocks located between the tram (trolley) running through the main streets in Amsterdam. More often than not, tram service was put on hold, providing the Amsterdam citizens chances to steal more blocks for their wood burning stoves.

Of course, I knew Johnny lied. He'd stole it. Johnny cleverly hid it in our coal shed for he knew very well he'd get in trouble with Mother. Eventually, the wooden block was used and enjoyed for its warmth as well as to prepare a cooked meal.

Now, it had become very quiet in the home. My thoughts traced back to everything that had occurred during the day. I wondered if Agatha was still crying or if maybe my father and her boyfriend had left. I felt a lump in my throat as I thought of her. How could Agatha, my gorgeous cousin, have fallen in love with a German?

"Johnny," I whispered. "Do you think she's a traitor?"

"Who?" was his grumpy answer. "Go to sleep. It's okay."

Half-awake and half-asleep, my thoughts switched from the present back into the past. The fun bike rides with Agatha with me on the back of her bike and her long, blond hair blowing in the wind, tickling my nose. She'd peddle all the way to the outskirts of Amsterdam to one of her favorite places called Aalsmeer, a quaint village where in April tulips were in full bloom in all shapes and colors. Sometime later, the bulbs would be harvested and then exported to almost every corner of the world. All this fun with our cousin was about to be stopped by Mama when she found out Agatha had taken me along with her to a German administration building in search of her German boyfriend who worked there.

Once we had arrived, Agatha dropped me off at the front entrance of the office building. Never had I seen so many soldiers gathered in one particular place, barely giving a glance in my direction. Luckily, Agatha had left her umbrella with me as a promise she'd only be a moment. Clouds had gathered and the wind had picked up with a sprinkle of rain or two hitting the pavement below. Huddled in a corner on the top of the stairs, I had shielded myself from the enemy with Agatha's open umbrella. From there, the only moving thing in my sight were the black shiny boots going up and down the steps of this dreaded enemy. They seemed like huge black snakes ready to attack. Agatha kept her promise, though. It had not been long before she came out of the building whisking me away from this awful place.

Sleep still had not come. Once again, my thoughts traveled back into the past to another important person. My school mate, Sonja. Memories of her took me away to the first day when we finally got acquainted.

This is when the old man helped Ada find her way home after she went looking for her friend, Sonja, and couldn't find her. Sketch done by Ada's husband, Don.

Chapter Four

SONJA

Sonja, a pale and shy girl, kept mostly to herself. She had large, dark eyes that seemed enormous on her small, thin face framed with dark, shiny hair pulled back into long, pretty braids. It occurred to me, more than once, that she was always standing alone watching the other children who were ever so busy with jumping rope at recess time.

Much was happening on the street where Sonja and I attended school. We had a rather unique playground which was only the sidewalk in front of the school. It was very wide, with lots of room for many children to play. Our school was called the Spiegelschool, located in one of the busiest parts of Amsterdam Centrum.

Though Sonja seemingly preferred being left alone at the school grounds at recess time, she could by no means be bored for our group of school buddies made sure our new friend would be included in all our games. When we got tired of jumping rope or playing kickball, we'd take time out, which meant going in one of the two large apartment buildings three levels high. These buildings stood at either side of the school. Both buildings had steep, wide marble steps providing a wonderful hiding place and a chance to share gossip or to plan a bit of mischief.

My favorite place to sit was on the window sills of the ground level apartments. Sonja must have found it just as pleasant, watching the hustle and bustle of the traffic in the busy street from her perch.

There were trolley cars commuting back and forth at a constant pace and scores of bicycle riders making their debut every morning on their way to work, creating a symphony of bells as the impatient riders signaled for the slower traffic to yield. I had finally made up my mind that this girl had been lonely long enough. So, as long as the decision had been made, I decided not to waste any more time. Carefully, I approached her as if not to scare away this delicate creature. I sensed her surprise at first, but soon enough, we were chattering away about a million things.

I found her to be so sincere that I immediately liked her. I was happy with my new-found friend and couldn't wait to get home to tell Mother about her. Mother only listened with half an ear, not because she wasn't interested, but, like so many people, she had so much to worry about.

It was early winter in 1944, what would be the last year of the war. Food had become even scarcer as more and more of the farmer's harvest were sent to the German troops. Mother's main worry was where the next meal for our family would come from.

My friendship with Sonja continued. We would jump rope together until we thought we'd drop. When we tired of that, we would play acrobat on the chain stretched between two metal posts located on the corner of our block near the Spiegelschool.

One sunny day, at Sonja's invitation, I walked her home. I was invited to come in for a while. Her parents were very kind, but it surprised me that they seemed so much older than my parents. Sonja's father looked like an old fashioned college professor in his brown suit and rather heavy beard. His quick smile entranced me. I liked and trusted him immediately.

He caught me staring at him while I was wondering if he was going to be one of Hitler's victims. As though he could read my mind he asked, "Do you like the Germans?"

"Oh, no!" I replied. "I don't like those scary soldiers."

He smiled at me and I knew I had made a friend by my reply.

Sonja's mother made very little effort to be sociable. Sonja made up for her mother's silence, chattering away a hundred miles an hour. Then, her father interrupted her and suggested I'd better start for home.

I remember so well Sonja's father apologizing for not being able to offer me refreshments. I assured him I didn't expect anything and I wasn't hungry. Of course, he knew this was the biggest fib he'd heard in a long time. It is a very important custom in Holland to make visitors feel welcome and refreshments, in the form of coffee or tea with little cakes, were always offered. It was apparent it bothered them that they couldn't follow up on this all-important custom.

After I said my good-byes to Sonja's parents, I promised her I'd see her again the following day in school and then I left.

I was happy to be on my way home. Darkness came on soon in winter and curfew time had been set back to an earlier hour. It wasn't difficult finding my way back home. The familiar canals and those wonderful bridges which I dearly loved were soon in sight. From there, it was only a few minutes to my home. Mother hadn't even missed me, for she was used to me stopping at my other friend, Lucie's house, so she didn't question my being late.

Sonja's gentleness and kindness made for a comfortable friendship. She'd often look up from her schoolwork to exchange a quick smile while sitting at our wooden school desks in our classroom. At recess, I would share my secrets with her and tell her about Casey, a boy at school who I had a terrible crush on. She agreed eagerly with me when I told her the girl named Greta, who Casey had a crush on, was chubby.

Summer had been replaced by a very cold, rainy, bleak fall. It became necessary for the students at the elementary school to stay in at recess time because of the bad weather. This was the time when our gymnastics room was utilized more than in the summer. We would race to see which one of us could reach the dressing room, located in the corner of the large gym, first. Sonja would never win. I simply wouldn't allow it, after all, my other friend, Lucie, would never let me win. Winning wasn't hard. It was just that Sonja didn't have the energy and spunk I had. She was sluggish climbing the ropes. She'd barely be a foot off the floor when I had already reached the top looking down at her. The stretch bars really turned her off, which was hard for me to imagine. That room brought me closer to heaven on earth than I could have ever hoped for. But, Sonja made up for her lack of interest in the gym when she was jumping rope with me. She was the best.

One morning, when I waited for her as usual by the large wooden doors in front of the school, she was late. I waited as long as I dared, but the second bell had already rung and I knew being late meant a visit to the principal's office. The principal was seldom seen, so to us he was mightier than mighty. To be late for class was the unforgiving sin only excused by him. My heart would skip a beat just thinking of the possibility of having to face him.

I felt lost without Sonja and realized how much I had depended on her friendship. I kept a vigil on the classroom door hoping she would walk in at any moment. The teacher looked at me knowing something was wrong. If she had any notion of what went on, she didn't let on.

My mother's words echoed through my mind. "Those poor Jews. I don't understand."

Whenever the Jewish situation was brought up, her frustration would start all over again.

My fears became even stronger when Sonja missed the following day of school. As my mind kept pondering on what could possibly keep Sonja way from school, I realized something had to be done. I made myself a promise that as soon as the bell rang dismissing school for the day, I'd go find her. I assured myself even if I was only at her house once, I could certainly find it again.

The hours in the day went by very slowly. At last, the bell rang and school was dismissed. I shoved my way out as fast as I could and was on my way. Every minute counted, I told myself, knowing it would be dark soon. Since school let out at 4:00 p.m., it was only an hour away from sunset. Mother would certainly be worried if I wasn't home before dark.

Walking at a brisk pace kept me from being cold. I crossed the busy street (De Overtoom) the school was located on and approached a small park I had to cross through to reach my final destination. This park bordered the large, main canal, De Nassau Kade, a familiar place to me because it was a regular route to church every Sunday and a favorite place to go walking. Soon, I was at a busy intersection in Amsterdam—a main point where all the trolleys running through town would meet.

The opera house came into sight. Every Sunday, I'd marvel at the splendid building and my imagination would run astray with me. I'd imagine myself as one of the fancy dressed ladies arriving in horse-drawn coaches, escorted by a handsome man into the beautiful structure. My friend, Lucie, and I had watched the people come many a night. With every beautiful woman that would exit her lovely carriage, we'd imagine ourselves in a dress prettier than hers and, without a doubt, we'd be the most stunning of all the fairy maidens that ever set foot in here.

Today was not a day for day dreams, though. This was reality and a heavy burden for a child so young. It was a long way to the Leidse Street, but from there I knew the way to Sonja's home.

It was still busy with people returning home from work. The canals with their wonderful bridges were in sight; a welcome landmark. It wouldn't be long now before I'd arrive at Sonja's house. I looked at the houseboats on the canal from the bridge I had just crossed. How wonderful, I thought, to live in one of those. One could simply lift anchor and sail away from the hardships of this war. I laughed at my own absurdness and increased my pace as time was passing quickly. The second bridge I needed to cross was the Blue Bridge, a duplicate of one built in France many centuries ago. I had learned in school that in comparison with the Dutch, who are a very practical people and kept their architecture plain, the French people were quite ornate. This beautifully-designed bridge spanned the largest canal, the Amstel, in Amsterdam. It was certainly a testimonial to the French and had been the pride of every Amsterdammer for centuries.

At last, I arrived where Sonja lived. The street was long with a solid block of apartments which all looked the same from the front. So, I knew finding the right one was going to be a challenge. I had pretty well covered the whole length of the street when all of the sudden, I remembered my first visit to Sonja's house when I first met her Jewish family. Her place had the shiniest brass doorknob of all the others. My heart pounded with anticipation as I spotted the right apartment. Quickly, I stepped up to the door and, with a shaky hand, I knocked and waited anxiously for a response. When no answer came, I knocked again, only much harder this time, hoping the first knock had not been loud enough. After many tries, I realized no one was going to open the door for me, and quite possibly, for no one ever again.

This terrible war had reached out its long, bony fingers and gripped us with its cruel clinch, like it had so often done. This evil forced me to part with my friend, whom I dearly loved. I felt hate for the first time in my life.

Tears of fright and the unknown whereabouts of my friend turned into tears of uncontrollable anger. I stepped away from Sonja's front door looking up at the upstairs window in hopes I could possibly be mistaken and at any moment her face could appear in the window. It became more and more difficult to extinguish those feeling of hope. Soon, those held on feelings of hope were shattered when I noticed that dreadful word JODEN (Jews) roughly painted in big black letters on Sonja's door. With clenched fist, I pounded as hard as I could on that haunting word JODEN.

"Make it go away" I said, sobbing. "Oh, make it go away." With my voice trailing off, I fell on my knees. In a tear-choked soft whisper, I pleaded, "You can't have her. She's my friend."

I realized later on in my life that out of hate, courage is formed. That kind of courage had been part of the Dutch people challenged by wars fought through history; wars fought and finished with the Dutch as the victors.

I finally understood why it was necessary for my father to be away from home so much. I was proud of him. Yes, my father would have to help them. He had helped hide Jewish people before.

I quickly got up from the step where I had rested myself while pondering what to do next. I got up with such a jerk I nearly knocked a man off his bike as he was riding by.

"Oh, sir," I yelled at him. "Do you know Sonja who lives here?"

He turned his head toward me, gave me a casual look, and shrugged his shoulders. "No."

Well, I thought, *Father will fix things up anyway. He will save my friend from the awful fate of most Jews. This wouldn't be hard for him.*

It was getting darker, so it would be dangerous to linger any longer. I knew I had to hurry. Mother would be home by now from singing lessons. My mind was going on at a rapid pace wondering how Father was going to help Sonja and her family. Then, with a jolt, I realized I had taken a wrong turn. My landmarks—the canals—were nowhere in sight.

I felt tears coming on again. The sun was setting lower and lower by the minute and it was beginning to get so cold. Every block I walked, I hoped that by reaching the end of it and turning the corner, I'd see my beloved canals. The night scared me, but what frightened me even more was I would bump into one of those German soldiers. Most everyone was inside by now since curfew time was near. I felt hopeless. The nightfall made everything look scary. I finally burst into tears, not being able to hold back.

Unexpectedly, I felt a gentle touch on my shivering shoulder and a gentle voice asked, "Why the tears?"

I glanced up into a smiling face. One that quickly turned into a puzzled look. I blurted out my story to this kind, concerned man who took my hand and secured it into his own. My tears swiftly vanished and I felt safe once again. I explained about my canals, describing the Blue Bridge, which made me feel upon seeing it as a huge welcome home sign. He grinned with understanding.

We were soon there.

He asked, "Can you find your way home from here?"

"Yes, sir," I said with new-found confidence. "I won't need you anymore. Thank you." I watched him go on his way. He glanced back and waived for the last time before he turned the corner.

I walked fast until it turned into a run, right past the opera house and across the bridge that led into my park. I never appreciated this lovely park more than I did that evening, even though it was quite empty now. The benches were vacant with not even a bird in sight anywhere. The area itself was a friendly site in spite of the empty darkness. When passing the newspaper stand, I knew it must be past 6:00 p.m. because it had been closed up already. The pigeons who generally scampering around the benches foraging for something to eat had also called it a night and were huddled under the benches for shelter against the cold.

Leaving the park area, I started running again, past my friend, Lucie's, house, going and going. In spite of my frantic hurry, I couldn't help but think if Lucie were running with me, I'd have a good chance of winning this race.

Oh, it felt so good to be home. I didn't waste a minute telling my parents the whole story. How badly my father wished he could have helped me find my best friend. The best he could do was to ensure me that our friendship would continue someday in another dimension.

After a restless night, thinking of Sonja and knowing what quite possibly had happened to her and her family, morning did finally arrive.

***

I heard Mother in the kitchen preparing our breakfast. Due to the lack of milk, breakfast meant a watery porridge. Mother had spent her last ration coupons on milk a few days ago. Coupons for milk were only given to those families who had infants or young children. For a short period during the war, we'd had milk for our breakfast.

There was a great deal of noise in the kitchen being made by our round-cheeked, two-year-old brother, Martin, demanding more food by hitting his spoon hard on the marble-topped table. This woke up Johnny.

"Oh, he's at it again," Johnny grumbled.

Everyone recognized Martin's demands. Mother would often say, "I can't seem to fill his tummy full enough to make him happy."

"Hey, Sis," Johnny said, being full awake now, "Let's ask Mother what happened to the soldier."

We pretty well scared our mother to death while almost breaking down the kitchen door being the first one in. In one breath we both asked, "What happened to the soldier guy?"

Putting down the spoon she was stirring another portion of porridge with, she answered with a big smile and said, "He's gone, kids. Father took him away. We won't need to worry about that matter anymore. Remember, don't say a word about this to anyone. It could mean trouble for all of us if— "

Not being able to finish, Johnny interrupted. "Where did Father take him? Where did he go?" His eyes were wide in excitement when he asked, "Did he shoot him?

"Johnny," Mother protested. "Your Father wouldn't do such a thing."

"Oh, why not?" he asked bravely. "He's just a German."

I knew he'd get us in trouble with that statement.

Mother recognized the Germans to be the enemy, but to her, they were still human beings to be treated with human kindness. "Shame on you, son. Sit down and eat your breakfast. Father took him away as I already told you... to a safe place." Her explanation concerning our unexpected guest satisfied both of us.

Drawing of a Holland windmill by Ada's husband, Don.

Chapter Five

The Printing Press

Typing the underground bulletins one-by-one had become quite time consuming because of the increasing demand for them. Somehow or somewhere Father got hold of a antique printing press.

The much-needed printing press was smuggled into our home in Amsterdam West. It was in working order, much to the delight of Father. There must have been someone who knew how to operate the printing press because it was fully functional soon after it was delivered to our home.

I personally helped out by taking turns cranking a handle to set it in motion.

Soon, it became too dangerous to keep it in our home.

So, Father took the printer apart bit-by-bit. Since he had a falsified pass allowing him to be on the street after curfew, it gave him the chance to transfer the printing press to the basement of the office building where he worked. The basement hadn't been used in years. Old files were kept there and not much else.

Father could speak good German, so whenever he was stopped by a soldier or a policeman, he would very bravely tell them he was on his way to the office with repair parts for workplace machinery. Father had a great sense of humor and made good use of it. The few times he was stopped by either the Dutch police or the Nazis, he'd pull one of his black market cigars out of his pocket and offer it to the unsuspected enemy. Soon, he was on his way again and out of a situation that could have had serious consequences.

The printing press was quickly put together and out of harm's way and the resistance would continue to distribute its information.

***

I don't remember how often the contacts would come to pick up news bulletins from our home, but it was often enough to bring attention to a neighbor who lived right across our street on the third floor of the building.

She was an older lady who hardly ever left her apartment. Having nothing better to do, she was rather curious about what was going on at our home, since we had people coming and going. The café style curtains at her windows were always pushed aside with her peeking out at the street below. This became a concern for our parents. Especially when she had a regular, special visitor—a German soldier who was chauffeured in a limo-type car. He must have been someone higher up in the German army.

Perhaps he was a family member. Could he have been her son?

Whatever the case, she never turned us in.

It could be that her family member had also been drafted like our neighbor's husband. Or, maybe she just didn't have the heart to turn us in because we kids were always playing on our sidewalk.

Whatever the reason, we were very grateful to her.

I don't know what happened to her.

She suddenly disappeared one day. We suspected maybe her son got her out of the country in time. If she was a German citizen and he may have brought her back to Germany. During war time, many people simply went missing and were misplaced, leaving friends and family with no answers to their whereabouts. We could only speculate and hope for good results.

Spiegelschool as it was when Ada visited in 1985.

Chapter Six

DODIE

Dodie was Father's secretary who happened to be a bit of an old maid. Born in Belgium, she'd never been married and moved to the Netherlands in her early thirties.

She was a woman of courage and could be counted on whatever the challenge was to be. This, of course, made her a much desired candidate for the underground movement with Father's group.

At one point in time, it became necessary for some important information to change hands to another connection in the resistance group. Dodie agreed to be the go-between. It must have been a message of great concern because it had been decided for me to go along with her delivering the papers. Having a child on the back of her bike would help her look like she was taking her child to the park or school.

All went well for part of the bike ride with Dodie, but when we arrived close to the Queen's Palace in the inner city of Amsterdam, a rather large group of soldiers, together with the Dutch police, were in the process of stopping people and asking for I.D. papers.

Dodie became scared, knowing it could become more than just asking for identification. She turned quickly into a surviving mode. There was a bar located right next to us on the same side of the street we were on.

Thankfully, the pub was empty of the regular German customers. Only a surprised barkeep welcomed us with a puzzled look on his face. Without saying a word, he pointed at a place where Dodie could park her bike. A makeshift area in a far corner of the pub had been provided for his regular customers. They were mostly from the general population and were very few consisting largely of Dutch citizens who'd joined the Nazi party, the NSB (National Socialistic Party) whom were given extra privileges like socializing in pubs around the city of Amsterdam and beyond.

"Where are all your customers?" Dodie asked, trying to muster up a smile. She ignored the shouts coming from the outside penetrating the silence inside the pub.

"Well, it's only noon, a bit early for business," he answered with the same puzzled look on his face. "Don't get to wait on real ladies much anymore since this place has become a hangout for the Germans. What can I get you and you're your little partner here?"

"This is my niece," Dodie lied. "I'll have a beer, thank you, and a ginger beer for her."

Dodie made herself comfortable on one of the barstools. After a few tries, I climbed on one beside her. Too frightened to say a word, I watched and listened to our brave Dodie striking up a conversation with the barkeep.

It seemed to please him to have an ordinary, loyal Dutch citizen in his pub who he could relate to. "About what's going on outside here," he assured Dodie. "It happens many times in this busy part of our city. It's just Germans flexing their muscles trying to frighten the citizens."

By this rather bold and dangerous accusation toward the enemy, Dodie seemed to feel the good spirit coming from this man. "Guess they are looking for more Jews to arrest."

"Jews? Not hardly. Those poor folks have pretty well all been transported to the concentration camps by now."

I didn't hear what he murmured after his comment on the Jews, but judging from his body language and his visible compassion for the Jews indicated he could be trusted. With a good hard slap with his towel on the pub counter, he said with a softer tone of voice, "A beer for my lady customer and a ginger beer for her niece... coming up."

"Are you okay?" Dodie asked, giving me attention I so desperately needed by this time. "Don't worry, I think he's a good man," she said. "Good people are so often put in bad situation in wartime."

"You mean he's not a German lover?"

"No, no I doubt that," Dodie said with a little smile.

I felt relieved by the trust she felt coming from the open and honest attitude of the barkeep. With the war coming closer to being won by the Allies, the Dutch attitude of hostility against their enemy had slowly emerged out in the open in the streets and in public places. All too often their enthusiasm would turn into bold consequences.

"Glad you came in," the barkeep said good-naturedly. "As I mentioned before, it has been a long time since I served a real lady. Oh, excuse me..." he winked in my direction. "I'll correct that... *two* ladies."

This deserved a big smile coming from both of us. Dodie gave him a look of appreciation while sipping away at her beer.

"Try your drink," urged Dodie. She pushed the ginger beer closer to me. "It used to be one of my favorite treats growing up. It's made with real sugar."

Anxious to please her, I took a sip. I decided it was not going to be one of my favorite childhood memories. It tasted sweet and spicy, oh how I wished this could have been a glass of milk instead.

"Like it?"

Before I had to answer her question, the barkeep closed his cash register with a loud bang after she had paid him.

"Dodie," I whispered. "Is he a good guy?"

"Yes, he is. A little noisy, perhaps."

We both watched him busily engaging himself preparing for the afternoon customers. The noise of the turmoil from outside had quieted down.

"Are we going to leave soon, Dodie?"

"Yes, sweet one, as soon as the trucks leave with the soldiers. Now, you can help me by listening closely for the truck motors to start and then we will leave, I promise."

The barkeep picked up on Dodie's conversation, prompting him to come over on our side of the bar. With another concerned look on his face, he placed himself right in front of us.

"Look lady," he said. "I don't know what your reason is for being here in my bar and it is certainly none of by business to interfere, but I have a feeling you need to leave as soon as this outside commotion is over. This could become a dangerous place for you and the kid to be in."

Dodie played close attention to his warning. She hurried and finished her beer and then ordered me to finish mine, as well.

"Can't," I complained.

"Why? What's wrong?"

"I can't finish it. Sorry, Dodie, but I have an awful stomach ache."

"What did you have to eat this morning? Anything?" asked Dodie in a concerned voice.

"No, no one did. Mother told us to drink some water. She said that would take the hungry feeling away."

"Oh, my word," Dodie said with a gasp. "Spicy ginger beer on an empty stomach? Where's the bathroom? Sir, could we use it, please?"

The barkeep pointed at a door next to the back exit. "Go ahead," he said. "It's not locked."

It only took a few moments before relief came. I had been in dreadful discomfort spurred on with Dodie's nervous reaction. A knock on the bathroom door was followed with many more.

"Are you done yet?" Dodie asked over and over again. "Are you crying? Oh, I am sorry. I didn't mean to make you cry. Just hurry, okay?"

It was difficult keeping the tears from coming, but I also knew I had to be brave for Dodie. The barkeep at this point joined in with a more convincing way to help me with my tummy ache.

"Little partner," he said. "I have something for you to help your tummy ache feel better."

My curiosity got the best of me. When I came out of the restroom, he handed me a couple of breadsticks. "This is for you. Can't have a little lady like you going hungry."

I looked up at a teary-eyed Dodie and asked, "May I eat this?"

"Of course," she said wiping at my face. "It will help you feel better. Why didn't you tell me you were hungry?"

"I would have, but Mama said I mustn't complain because everyone is hungry."

There was a moment of profound silence. Suddenly, the sound of roaring truck motors filled the afternoon air outside the pub.

"The trucks of the Germans!" I cried. "Dodie, they are leaving. Can we, too?"

"All right." She smiled. "Get ready."

The barkeep looked at me. "Tummy ache gone?"

"Oh yes, and thank you for the breadsticks. They were delicious."

"*Graag gedaan,*" he said with a warm grin. (Given with pleasure). "Now, listen," he said, pulling me closer to him. "Remember to be a good and obedient partner for Dodie here. Will you do that?"

"Yes, I will. I already promised my mama and papa."

"Okay then, next time we meet I'll have more breadsticks for you, minus the ginger beer."

"Yes sir!"

Dodie thanked our benefactor for the safe temporary shelter he had provided for us.

"Hurry now while they are leaving," he urged. "Here, here. Let me get your bike for you. Open the door, little partner. Most everyone has left. I think you are safe to go. Be safe."

With one last look of gratitude, we parted. We went outside the pub closing the door softly behind us.

"Hop on," she said nervously pointing to the back of her bike. She tucked away the documents making sure they were still in their proper place and then, with a grunt of approval, she started out to finish our mission.

Her tenseness affected me to the point where I felt like I needed to be included in what was going to happen next.

"Where are we going, Dodie?"

"Be still Ada," was her impatient response. The extra weight in back of her bike while peddling up a slight hill caused her to breathe in heavy, rapid spurts. Her face was red and sweaty when she turned to give me a reassuring smile. "We are going to deliver some papers to a nice family. It shouldn't be much longer now until we get there."

"How long, Dodie?"

"Umm, twenty minutes."

"So, you do know where we are going?" I worriedly asked.

"Well, of course I do. Relax."

I had to back off. I noticed her tone of voice was tense. I kept my word and left her to her own thoughts.

"We are going to stop at that park up the road a ways and sit down for a spell, okay?" She peddled on barely having enough strength to make it going up the hill.

I was sure she hadn't had much to eat this morning. Lack of nourishment meant lack of strength. Compassion for her overwhelmed me at that point. My grip on her tightened as I held on to her waist. A gentle breeze blew through her hair touching my forehead followed with a faint scent of perfume as my cheek touched the back of her shoulder. Just for a moment, I felt some embarrassment having held on to her so tightly. I straightened giving more attention to the lovely country side. This could have been such a wonderful day in the country while soaking up the warm rays of the sun. After a series of chilly spring days, the sun had finally come out warming the weather as well as lighting the spirit of a rather devastated Dutch population.

My thoughts were suddenly interrupted when Dodie came to a screeching halt.

"Time out," she said wearily.

We had reached the park that we used as a rest stop.

"I'll hold the bike," she said. "You get off, careful don't fall."

Dodie helped me get down. It gave me the chance to overlook the rest stop more closely. It was a great little place with a few benches, two rather worn tables, and a covered sandbox.

"We could make sand castles, Dodie" I joked.

"Not today, little girl," she joked back.

After the inspection of the place, we both sat down on the bench closest to the edge of the country road that was almost totally deserted. We could see a person here or there, walking their dogs or an over-the-fence conversation when we had passed a home or two. A friendly farmer passed by us with a horse drawn trailer lugging a huge load of hay.

"Going to Germany, I suppose," Dodie said and snorted in disgust. "Can't stay too long. We still have a mile to go. Do you feel up to it?" she asked with a wink thrown in my direction.

I was glad she changed the subject. Talking about Hitler's wrong doings could get so depressing. Sitting next to her on the park bench gave me a safe feeling. I decided while looking up at her that I really liked her features. They were somewhat plain, but her lovely hair that she wore partly pulled back and fastened with two lovely pearl studded combs made up for her ordinary, but sweet face.

Dodie sensed I was studying her, but she allowed me to do so. Suddenly, she pulled me closely toward her. "Here," she said. "Put your head on my shoulder."

"Why? What..." I stammered.

She withdrew a rather large handkerchief out of her purse and said, "Put it in front of your mouth and don't say a word. Don't look up. Just act like you are in pain."

I tugged the handkerchief away from my mouth and wondered if she'd gone mad.

"Do what I tell you!" she hissed at me.

Instantly, I knew what was on her mind and what made Dodie behave the way she did. To my horror, I heard the sound of two motorcycles in the distance of the country road coming in our direction driven by two Nazis.

"*Moffen,*" I shouted. It was a degrading Dutch term for German soldiers. "Or, maybe they're SS. Dodie, what are we going to do? We need to run."

"They are not the SS, thank goodness," she said. "Calm down, girl. Just keep that hankie in front of your mouth and act like you are in pain."

I could feel the terror coming. She seemed surprisingly calm. The roar of the two motorcycles became louder as they got closer to us. I dug my face into Dodie's coat holding onto her for dear life.

"Oh, they are getting so close. Are they going to take us away, Dodie?"

With a tight embrace she assured me, "Not if you are going to do exactly what I told you to do." She looked me straight in the face and added, "I trust you to be my partner. Remember our talks in the pub about sticking together no matter what?"

With this sweet reminder, she kissed me on top of my head and gave me a good bear hug. The soldier was just minutes away from reaching the little rest stop.

"*Moffen*, all right," said Dodie bitterly.

Hurriedly, she slipped the scrolled up papers into my coat pocket. When I protested, she placed her hand in my pocket and explained, "They won't search a child, so leave them there. Just keep my handkerchief in front of your mouth and look like you are in pain, okay?"

"Ya, ya, I know. Maybe they'll even pass us by." I couldn't be convinced everything was going to end up all right. "Dodie," I whined, "If they find this I my pocket, I know they are going to shoot me dead."

In spite of the ever potential danger we may be in, she couldn't help chuckling at my hysterics. All hopes that they would simply pass by vanished when we heard their vehicles slow down and eventually come to a stop right in front of our bench.

"Be good now," she whispered at me. "Do as I told you and you'll be fine."

The two soldiers shut off their motorcycles and for a long moment, they just sat there and stared at us.

Dodie managed a smile.

Oh, dear. If she greets these jerks with a "Heil Hitler," I will kick her so bad...

The younger of the two soldiers loosened the straps of his helmet and got off his motorcycle, walking right over to us. "*Guten morgen, Fräulein,*" he said cheerfully, greeting us good morning.

"Good morning to you, sir," responded Dodie rather curtly.

"Why are you sitting so alone here?" he asked in broken Dutch. It was a friendly enough question.

Encouraged by his pleasant attitude, Dodie answered his question casually, "My niece and I are taking out a few moments to rest ourselves. Thank you."

I took a closer look at him. He seemed so young, maybe nineteen or twenty years old. He took off his helmet and gloves. His hands were slender and appeared to be soft. He was certainly no farmer from the country, I thought. His dark blond hair matched the blue of his eyes that were set in a very handsome face. "Beware of sheep in wolves clothing," I could hear Father saying in my head. It was almost surreal that someone so human as this soldier could be part of this evil regime. To our relief, we came to the conclusion these men were not part of the dreaded SS.

The other soldier finally joined in. He had a hard look about him, that of a battle beaten soldier. Glancing at him, I felt a lot less brave than I did a few minutes before.

"Stand up!" this one gruffly demanded of Dodie.

I let go of her, but kept the handkerchief tightly on my mouth.

He pushed the younger soldier, who stood close to Dodie, rudely to the side. He pulled Dodie toward him and started searching her. Her purse was thrown on the ground spilling her meager belonging. He was obviously disappointed, for his search didn't come up with anything he might have hoped for.

Pointing at my trembling body, he said in a much softer tone of voice than before "What's wrong with her?"

"Sir," Dodie said in her same polite manner as before. "My niece has a terrible toothache."

His face was full of sympathy now.

"We hope to find a dentist in Aalsmeer." Aalsmeer was a small town near Amsterdam.

This was now my opportunity to do my part. I looked up at him trying to seem as if I were racked with pain, even managing a little whimper or two.

"Sit down!" he told Dodie, giving her a rude shove toward the bench. The soldier moved in my direction then pointed at his mouth with a painful expression and nodded in sympathy.

Without another word being said, the two climbed back onto their motorbikes and left.

Dodie swiftly got off the bench to join me. We were both too stunned to say a word. Then, Dodie stated laughing nervously as the soldiers were speeding away.

We embraced each other in disbelief. She started to laugh again when she noticed I was still clutching the handkerchief against my mouth.

"You can take that off your face now," she teased. "Oh, *meisje* (girl), I could not have been more proud of you even if I tried. Such a performance you gave. It was so convincing even I became to believe you had a toothache."

"Really Dodie? I did good?"

"Yes, you did," she assured me. "Stay put." She pointed to the bench. "I want to show you something."

I watched her search for something around the bushes and trees. "What are you looking for, Dodie?"

"Just watch," she said. She picked up a sturdy branch from off the ground and wrote a large F in the soft dirt located next to the country road. "That's what it is all about, little girl" she said and then as she went on to say with a defiant tone of voice, "Ada, do you know what this letter 'F' stands for?"

"Dodie, I don't know… maybe French fries?"

With a roar of laughter coming from her she hollered, "Freedom!"

"Oh," I stammered. "Guess I should have known that."

"No, no, it's okay, my dear, brave, little friend. Someday you will come to understand the true meaning of what this word stands for. Yes, you will and soon, very soon."

Dodie finally relaxed.

With a great sigh of relief, we both watched the two soldiers disappear in the distance who were by now two small specks on the horizon far removed from us.

It was time to go and finish what Dodie had been assigned to do. I hopped on back of her bike when we were ready to go, but before we got on our way, she looked at me with that toothy smile of hers and said with a voice full of pride and satisfaction, "You know, *meisje*, do you realize we have outmaneuvered two soldiers who belong to the greatest army the world has ever known?"

I relished in her happiness for the moment. At this point I felt very close to my friend and protector. I handed her back the small scroll of paper containing the secret information we so carefully guarded. With renewed energy after the encounter with the enemy, the rest of our travel went on without further disruptions. Dodie and I located the contact she had been assigned to whom had been anxiously waiting for her delivery.

It had been a mission well accomplished.

And, I helped!

Underground bulletin header.

Chapter Seven

HERMAN

Herman was one of my father's sons from a previous marriage and my half-brother. He was nicknamed Boy.

It was 1944 and Herman had just turned nineteen-years-old. He was a good looking, hardworking kid. It was a blessing he hadn't been picked up by the Nazis and sent to Germany to be forced to work in their weapon factories.

Father divorced Herman's mother years before the war started. His younger son, Robert, stayed with their mother, but Boy lived with us most of the war years, and before.

Boy and Robert loved my mother very much.

It was a blessing for us having Boy live with us for he would often hit the road looking for food for our family. He'd walk many miles into the farm communities. If the trains were running, he'd hop on them to appointed areas where it was rumored farmers were selling or trading for goods.

On his way home from his journeys, plans had been made before-hand for Father and me to meet the train at a certain spot where it had to slow down due to a bend in the road. Boy would open the train window and throw out in our direction whatever food he'd been able to purchase. The reason for this was oftentimes the Nazi soldiers would be waiting at the train station ready to confiscate the food people carried with them. Luckily, Father still had his bike in working order thanks to the falsified document Father and his group had made. The documents never expired, so Father always had a way to work at all the places he needed to go, plus the time to do repairs when needed.

Father would place the bag of food in between me and him on the bike concealing it as much as possible. Boy would generally find potatoes turnips, or winter carrots to buy. Those items were mostly available at the right price. There were many good-hearted farmers who didn't take advantage of those of us starving city folks by charging huge prices for food even though many of them did become rich during that last year of the war for that very reason.

The ride back to our home on the bike was risky because there was always the chance of being robbed of the food we carried. Even though our brother's trips to the farms were often, Father and I had never been robbed of our precious cargo.

On many occasions, Father, Boy, and I would take the tram, (trolley) if they were running, to the edge of Amsterdam where there were many wheat farms. The farmers there would leave much of the harvested wheat behind in the fields. They would do this knowing the city folks would come and harvest the wheat to feed their starving families. This was a fun time for me—as much as it could be—because we did this together as a family. A neat memory.

On one of Boy's trips to the country, he threw a bag of sugar beets out of the train window. It surprised Father and me, wondering what to do with these weird-looking things. Did we cook them and eat them or did we plant them in our garden?

"We'll ask your mother," Father said.

Mother knew exactly what to do with them, for she was raised in the country. She boiled them until there was nothing left but a sticky substance that tasted sweet.

Our harvest of wheat from the previous trip to the country had already been grounded in Mother's antique coffee grinder, waiting to be used for her sticky buns. The sticky buns were prepared with wheat flour, soda, salt, and water (there was no milk) and then formed into the size of a tennis ball. Mother then placed it in a cheesecloth and lowered it into a pan of boiling water until it was cooked through. She then drizzled some of the sugar beet substance on top of a slice of the cooked dough. As my memory would have it, it really tasted good.

The name of this cooked wheat ball was called "Jan in de Zak" (Jan in the bag), a recipe from long, long ago. It provided regular sustenance to feed our hungry bodies.

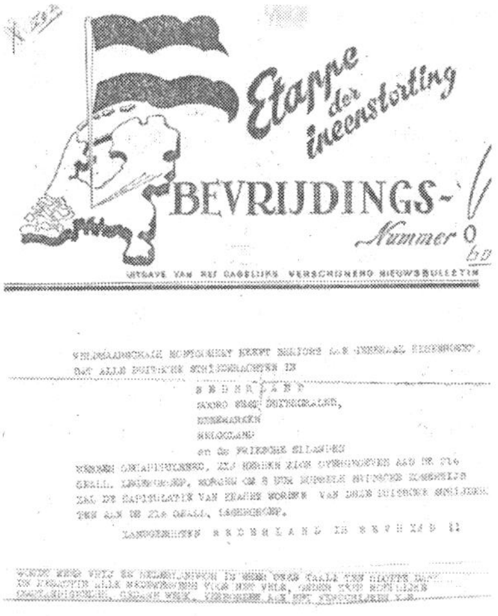
Etappe der ineenstorting

BEVRIJDINGS-

Nummer 0

The underground bulletin.

Chapter Eight

DODIE'S ARREST

It was Saturday morning and school was out for the weekend. November rain and wind had arrived with unexpected force much earlier than normal. 1944 had been a long, troublesome year, with more hardships still to come. The stress of a senseless year at war against a powerful enemy had confronted our parents with many worries and responsibilities.

Being the co-conspirator of a resistance worker started taking its toll on our mother. Her devotion to country, church, and family, combined with a strong testimony that there is a God in Heaven looking out for His righteous children had kept her will strong and enduring.

Father was totally dedicated to the "work," as he called it. He mostly spent the weekdays and nights in the hidden basement room at his office printing the BBC News Bulletins. Our regulars were more than eager for the news coming from England, for the Allies were right on our doorstep. News about the great offensive D-Day had filled us with hope. Father's antique printing press kept him and his comrades busier than ever before. Between his resistance work and holding an important calling as Branch President of the LDS (Mormon) Haarlem Branch, he had become almost a stranger in our home.

From the conversations between our parents, we realized, more than ever, the risk of Father being discovered. It put us all in great danger. On one such occasion when Father came home to spend the weekend with us, he seemed distant and concerned. Surprisingly, at this time, we were not sent to our rooms. At first, he resisted Mother's pressing him to share his concerns with her. After some kind persuasion coming from her, he ultimately gave in. Father's little family stood in complete silence with all eyes fixed on this tall, determined, handsome man, who knew no fear.

Oh, how his demeanor had now changed.

"Mama," he began. "I wanted to keep you from this, but I see it's only fair for you to know." He walked over to embrace her and spoke softly. "Dodie was arrested this morning by the SS." He was referring to the abbreviation of Schutzstaffel, the black-uniformed elite corps of political soldiers and police of the Nazi party.

Mother's face turned an ashen gray; an agonized parched sound escaped her throat. Somewhat abruptly, she pushed her husband aside and walked over to the front window to shut the heavy window drapes. She turned to Father in total frustration, her eyes wide with fear.

"Mama, no. I said *was* arrested. Sit down here, dear," Father said while pointing at the large, overstuffed chair.

Mother never took her eyes off him as she sat down.

"She was arrested," he said. "But, she was then released."

Mother clasped her hands in a gesture of great relief. Her eyes still focused on Father.

He went on to explain. "I haven't talked to her personally, but it appears someone turned her in, suspecting Dodie's involvement with the resistance. The SS themselves interrogated her... poor girl." His voice was now full of compassion, taking in the scene of his precious family in front of him. With a deep sigh, he once again continued, "I was told by one of our contacts working at the headquarters that she had been roughly handled."

The fear had deepened in Mother's face. She reached up to touch Father's arm. "John," her voice was shaky and her eyes shiny with tears. "Is Dodie all right?"

"Yes, yes, thank goodness, yes."

Mother's tears were now shed without holding them back. These were truly happy and meaningful ones, mingled with sobs of relief.

"Mama, I have to tell you the rest of this great blessing we've been given. Dodie is fine, but we need to be more careful than ever before."

Mother nodded in agreement, wiping her tears with Papa's handkerchief. "Oh no," she said with a giggle. "When was the last time you got yourself a clean handkerchief out of the linen closet?"

"Well, dear," he said, giving her with sideways glance. "I've always felt as long as you keep your sense of humor we won't have anything to worry about."

Mother dried her tears with the soiled hankie, took a deep breath, and gave a rather embarrassed smile. She then asked, "What is the good news, John?"

At that point, we four children were once again included to hear the rest of Dodie's scary experience. Father continued. "Dodie, as I mentioned, was arrested and gratefully released later with this information coming from our contact at the headquarters there. After many hours of interrogation, faking unawareness of their accusations and her involvement with us, she had come very close to crumbling underneath the brutal questioning. Luckily," Father continued, "it became time for another shift of interrogators who took the place of her tormentors from the first shift."

Mother was aghast by what her husband was telling her. She held baby Nola tightly in her arms. The rest of us stood silently by, sensing the great danger Dodie had faced.

Not a word was spoken as all eyes were on our parents. Even my brother, Martin, our spunky little two-year-old, stayed quietly underneath the old round table, covered with a huge tablecloth.

Breaking the silence, Mother asked, "Where is Dodie now?"

"Oh, sorry dear, as I said, the second shift had arrived for that late afternoon. According to our information source, the man in charge of the interrogation at the particular time happened to be a Dutch policeman. I guess they are brought in to assist in certain matters because so many Germans are called up to the front, defending their strong holds, since the Allies are moving in at a rapid pace."

"John, please!" protested Mother. "Back to Dodie... what happened after the Dutch policeman came in?"

"Yes, yes dear." Managing a bit of a smile, he continued. "Dodie, as you can imagine, was so very frightened by then. When the others came in and started questioning her, she started to cry. In the confusion of a hurried exchange in shifts, not one person in charge bothered giving information of why Dodie had been arrested." Father chuckled when he proceeded to tell what the officer asked Dodie. "'Why are you here?' he asked her." Then, Father's chuckle turned into a big smile, "Of course, she was not about to tell him any details of her arrest, so she just said, 'I don't know, but please, sir. Let me go home.' The officer shrugged his shoulder and said, 'Go.'"

"He said just go?" Mother asked in disbelief.

"He said just go," Father repeated. "Mama," he said, his voice husky. "Do you realize how the Lord has blessed us? You and I and our family... as well as Dodie and all those others who work with us?"

"Yes," Mother's voice now being but a spare whisper. "The children and I acknowledge these blessing in our evening prayers." A reverent silence followed after Mother's sincere and humble comment.

The next day, plans were made to disperse us with different family members until the danger of a possible second arrest had passed. I hated leaving my family.

"Mama," I cried. "I don't want to leave you. You need me here."

"Hopie," she said, "You need to be safe. It will only be for a little while."

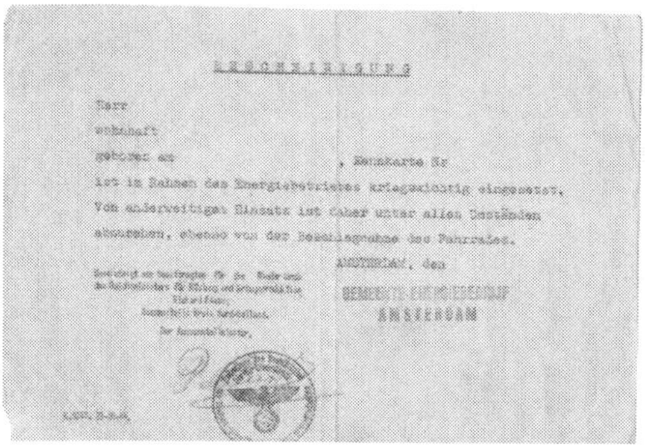

BESCHEINIGUNG

Herr

wohnhaft

geboren am , Kennkarte Nr

ist im Rahmen des Energiebetriebes kriegswichtig eingesetzt.

Von anderweitigem Einsatz ist daher unter allen Umständen abzusehen, ebenso von der Beschlagnahme des Fahrrades.

AMSTERDAM, den

AMSTERDAM

A false pass which the underground movement used.

Chapter Nine

DISPERSING

After Dodie's arrest, tension grew in our household. So many lives were at stake here, not only the members of the underground, but also their wives and children were endangered, as well. So, a decision had to be made.

Father decided that our "regulars," people who would gather the news at our home pertaining to the war, would have to be put on hold. Father had a well-planned, clever operation going. Part of it was gathering news from the BBC radio channel coming from England. The news about the war was recorded every day and then printed on sheets of paper with the aid of the very old newspaper press. The finished product had been given a name, *"De Estappe der in eens Storting,"* which translated to *The Epitaph of Destruction.* It was the only source of news the Dutch had access to about the war.

Scores of people would come to the house at a certain time of the day for this bulletin. Some of them donated money which enabled Father and his colleagues to buy black market food for the people who were hidden away in various places so the Germans would not find them. These were generally young men who were being forced to work in Germany factories.

Many young men were hauled away. Some of the lucky ones found places to hide with the assistance of the underground. As soon as our regulars were notified, it was decided that three of the four children in our family would be placed in the homes of family or friends.

Baby Nola stayed with Mother. My two brothers, Marty and John, were placed with family. I was placed in the home of our family doctor who had also been a close friend of Father's. This upset in the family routine took my mind off Sonja, as I was allowed to miss school for a few days. It must have been a relief for my parents knowing their children would be safe.

However, my experience in the house of our good doctor and his family was by no means a pleasant one. Their home was located on one of the beautiful canals in Amsterdam. The exterior of this magnificent dwelling had the typical look of a century old canal house with wide marble steps adorned with iron railings on each side that led up to the double oak front doors. The brass knocker on the door looked as if it must have just been polished as it gleamed in the sun. This was a sure indication of the cleanliness of the rest of the house.

I had been sent to the doctor's home without the escort of either parent. My heart pounded furiously as I hesitantly touched the gleaming knocker that looked like it was made of solid gold. The door opened slowly.

To my disappointment, it was not the friendly face of the doctor peering at me, rather it was the surprised face of one of the maid servants of the house.

"Come in, kid," she said as dismissively.

As I stepped into the corridor, I could feel a chill go down my spine. This place seemed like a museum and not a bit like the cozy home I had just left. The floors and walls were lovely, but they were also made of cold marble. The stairs leading up were elegantly carved of striking dark wood. What caught my attention immediately was the huge crystal chandelier that moved slightly in the draft as the maid closed the door behind us. As the sun shone through the leaded glass windows located on each side of the oak doors, it caught the brilliance of the hundreds of crystal pieces making up the chandelier. This created a sparkling and blazing mass of a thousand little explosions of light.

"*Kom Dan,*" the maid urged me on as she pointed to the door on the left.

The room I entered must have been a waiting area. It was decorated with large pieces of furniture. A round table was customary in Holland and placed in the middle of the room. Additionally, there was a small couch which sat between two large windows facing out over the street in front of the house. The ceilings were high, matching the age period of the structure. A huge wardrobe adorned the opposite wall of where the table was placed. It dwarfed the room, but it was beautiful in any case. The carpets were thick and comfortable to walk on. The table had been covered with a thick, rug type tablecloth, and, of course, there were the ever present oil paintings on the wall. My inspection of the room kept me occupied for quite a while, calming the rapid beat of my heart.

The maid entered the room. "Put your things here," she said as she pointed to the overnight case Mother had packed for me. I did as the maid asked me, placing the case in the corner of the room. "No, no," she insisted. "Put it behind the couch. It's less messy." Again I obliged her.

I took off my coat and handed it to her. She finally allowed herself to look at me a bit longer than the quick glances I had received before. As she took the coat, I detected a faint smile, but only in her eyes as her face didn't follow suit.

She had accepted the fact, I supposed, that I was going to be a guest in this house whether she liked it or not. Her smile was a start, though, and I was grateful for it.

I sat down on the settee and watched her as she closed the entrée door in order to open the coat closet next to it on the other wall. For a moment, my breathing stopped for on the top shelf of the coat closet were two of the most beautiful dolls I had ever seen. I could only look at them for as long as it took the maid to hang up my coat. My heart was pounding even faster than it had when I first knocked on the door of this glorious house.

The maid studied me thoughtfully, catching the excitement on my face. "Pretty, aren't they?" she asked softly.

I nodded my head as I was trying to get back to normal breathing.

"Don't you have a doll at home?" she asked.

"N-n-no," I stammered after I found my voice back.

She seemed surprised as she continued asking me questions. "Why not?" she asked.

"Well," I said. "I guess my mother just hasn't got the money to buy me one."

At that time, I honestly expected her to open the closet door, whisk the dolls off the shelf, and place them in my eager arms. Instead, she tossed her head to one side, shrugged her shoulders, and said, "I'll ask if you can play with them. Meanwhile, relax and keep real still."

She exited quietly, leaving me alone in this room where the only thing to keep me company was the ticking of the clock hanging on the wall. It seemed like hours before I would see anyone again. It had become dark outside and according to my companion, the clock, it was past supper time.

As my stomach started to growl, I wondered if they were going to share some of their food with me. My thoughts wandered as time passed. Was my mother making dinner? Is Mother keeping a close eye on our dear Hummus, the cat? Panic struck me as I visualized our pet going out unescorted. She'd sure to end up as some family's dinner tonight if care was not taken. Remembering how much Mother loved our dear Hummus put me at ease.

Thoughts of Sonja crept in my mind once more with endless thoughts of hope that perhaps someday she might still return. The agony of losing a beloved friend tugged endlessly at my heart. While thinking of her, I laid my head on the pillow on the couch. I wondered if perhaps this might be in poor taste, but my feet followed, not really caring if it was permitted or not. The maid had thoughtfully placed a small, woolen coverlet on the back of the couch, which I spread over myself.

Just as I got comfortable, the door opened and the maid came in, carrying a small tray. At a moment's glance, I noticed it had part of the family's evening meal on it. With the sight of food, I felt my hostile feelings against this servant and of the untouchable people, melt away.

"Hungry?" she asked. How absurd for her to ask me such a thing. The feeling of hunger was always there, nagging away. She had brought me soup with a large slice of dark bread.

I watched her every movement as I was anxious to get on with the meal. At last, she placed the tray in front of me on a small serving table she had brought along. I was so busy eating that I never noticed she had left the room. It was unforgivable of me not to have thanked her.

With my tummy full, I then laid my head down again on the fancy little pillow, tossed up my feet, and, once again, tucked the spread around myself with the ticking of the clock serenading me to sleep.

The clatter of rain against the window awoke me the next morning. As I looked around the strange surroundings, I was quickly reminded of where I was and the purpose for my being there. The rain sounded familiar and friendly. I watched the raindrops hit the window, then splatter on impact only to disappear into thin long streams of water down to the bottom of the sill. It seemed as though the panes were weeping a thousand tears for a multitude of sufferings.

As I observed with fascination at all these little raindrops, my thoughts again turned to Sonja. It wasn't long before I felt tears clouding my eyes.

The stage had been set. Loneliness and fear had taken its toll that morning. My eyes moved away from the window and focused on the coat closet where those coveted dolls were locked up. I imagined holding one, clutching it ever so tenderly against my chest. I wouldn't have to imagine that my rolled up pillow case was a real-life doll. Oh, how Mother would scold me when my pillow case was missing. Unexpectedly, the door opened abruptly and a tall, skinny, pimple-faced boy of about sixteen came in.

I immediately disliked him. He spoke in a rather abrupt voice. "So, you're the kid hiding from the Nazis, huh?"

I shook my head hard. I had been well indoctrinated by my parents to always deny anything when it came to dealing with the Nazis. "No." I then added, "They're not looking for me at all."

He dropped the subject. "Do you know how to stand on your head?" he asked to my surprise.

"Well, yes," I replied.

"Well," he grinned. "Let me see you do so."

I reluctantly got off the couch wondering if this was a joke or if he was serious. "Watch," he said as he moved the table somewhat to the side. "Watch," he said once more. He turned his head toward me to see if I was indeed observing. Then, thrusting his hands in front of him on the floor and throwing his feet up in the air, he stood in perfect form on his hands, touching his feet against the wall to keep his balance. "Can you do this?" he almost shouted.

"Oh, yes," I said calmly. "I can do this as well as many other acrobatic tricks."

"Well then," he said in a voice. "Show me."

Okay, here is my chance to show this skinny kid, who is obviously the son of our good doctor, that he has nothing over me.

Having always been the top student in my acrobatic class, I considered this stunt to be a piece of cake. I was eager to show him I could stand on my hands without having to touch the wall with my feet to keep me balanced. As I prepared to make the first move, showing him how it was really done, a funny feeling hit me.

Is this boy up to something?

He noticed my hesitation. "Come on," he urged. "Or, don't you really know how to do this?"

A split second later, I was standing in perfect form without the help of the wall keeping me balanced. Not until my dress fell down around my head did I realize how I had been tricked.

I could hear him laugh and laugh as he walked out of the room. I felt humiliated. How could I have fallen for this dumb trick? I threw myself down on the couch trying to hold back the tears as I watched the raindrops once more. Again, hours went by without anyone paying attention to their guest. How long was I to remain here in this unfriendly house?

My anger grew as I thought about my tormenter with the pimpled face. I kept a close eye on the entrance door, not knowing what to expect. The enemy wasn't only outside of this house, but inside, as well.

I missed my mom. I had visions of her dressing Nola who would never sit still long enough for Mother to finish with her. How upset and worried we all were when on one particular day, no one could find her anywhere. We looked all over the house and outside. We went up the street calling her name over and over. Mother finally discovered Nola underneath the table, hidden by a large tablecloth and eating a square of butter as fast as she could. The memory of her cute, round, little face, all covered with butter, still managed to bring a chuckle to the surface.

Mother didn't laugh, for butter was rationed to one square a week and only for children under three years of age. Poor Mother looked so forward to the square of butter once a week to fry a batch of pancakes, or better yet, to remind oneself of the taste of it. I laughed as I remembered how she had to pull Nola out from under the table and how hard that spunky sister of mine resisted. She was a greasy mess. Her cheeks were still glistening with the butter. She had been in such a hurry to eat it that she had missed her mouth completely. She would then use her apron dress to wipe her messy face.

"How am I going to get this butter out of her hair without soap?" Mama wailed. It was a struggled, but she managed.

Afterward, Papa reminded her Nola was only eating the butter she was entitled to.

"I know," Mama said with a sigh. "It's still a shame, though."

I could have entertained myself for the rest of the evening just reminiscing about the mischief my sister always somehow managed to get herself into. Then, sleep took over.

The next morning, spilling into the afternoon as well as the following evening was spent the same as the previous.

It was on the third day, early in the morning, when a distant sound of a vehicle broke the silence of the room. As the roar of the engine grew closer, I suspected this was not a passenger car approaching, rather a heavier vehicle like a truck. A fearful thought entered my mind.

Could the Germans have caught up with Papa? Did they make Papa tell them where his family is hiding? Do they know that I am here?

I looked around the room for a place to hide.

It made me shiver with fear that these hideous Nazi soldiers could be entering this very room at any moment, forcing me to go with them. Fear turned into panic and panic into desperation. I tried to formulate a plan of action. I had to somehow escape them.

All of a sudden, the sound of the engine stopped. I stood listening. Then, I slowly moved toward the window expecting to see them in front of the house. I felt my face flush and my mouth went dry. Thoughts of all sorts were racing through my head. But I knew what to do.

I'll get away.

With my plan organized, there was a sense of comfort. I moved the curtain very slightly as not to attract any attention of my presence in the house.

Surprisingly, there wasn't a person or vehicle anywhere in sight. Relieved beyond description, the awful fear of perhaps having to face the enemy left me.

A door slammed.

Shouts of orders were spoken in German.

I heard screams and pitiful cries of children.

I threw the curtain all the way back.

Just up the street, I could see the scene unfolding of one of the most inhuman cruel acts of this war—the rounding up of Jews.

They all wore the yellow Star of David sewn on their clothes. They were the helpless victims of war—the unwanted. I could almost hear my mother's words, "These poor people. Who knows what's going to happen to them."

How cruelly life has a way of revealing the truth to us, for at that very moment, I knew I would not ever see Sonja again. I cried the tears that hope and faith had been able to hold back all this time.

Without having realized her presence in the room, the maid had been standing behind me, witnessing this horror with me. Her arms held me carefully as she wiped away my tears with her apron.

"Your mother called," she said. "You're to go home."

Ada's family home in Amsterdam - #41

Chapter Ten

THE BIG ROBBERY

"Wake up, Sis! Wake up!"

I awoke with a start. "What?" I asked grumpily while tucking the blankets around me a bit tighter.

This year, 1944, had been recorded as the coldest winter in occupied Netherlands history. Germany had once again cut down our rations and we were particularly hit hard over the amount of coal we received every week. Mother had run out of coal days ago. Our little stove in the kitchen stood empty and unused. After school, we'd come home and just crawl into bed under the covers to keep warm or we would curl up in the overstuffed chairs with a blanket around us. When Mother had coal to burn, she would heat up water on her stove and spoil us with a hot water bottle.

Again, I heard my half-brother, Bobby, urging me to wake up. He was a reckless sixteen-year-old who had yet to come to the conclusion as to what the word "fear" meant.

Being seven years my senior, he always seemed so tall and grown up to me. Even though he had been staying with his own mother for a spell, he was no a stranger in our home. We truly loved his rather careless, good-natured personality.

He had, on two different occasions, robbed the Germans. The heist included many bags of rice and boxes full of loose tea. It was a happy day when Bobbie came home with a portion of his bounty for us all. We remember how happy our grandma was with her share.

"A warm cup of tea," she chanted over and over.

When Bobbie was finally forced to tell where he had found all this food, he then confessed. Knowing about the inventory of a certain school used by the Germans as a warehouse, he decided that he, too, needed some of the contents of it. He waited for evening to come before the first step was taken to fulfill his plan. When most of the guards had left their posts in the evening, and only a few had been left behind to guard the building, Bobbie made his move.

He sneaked through the back way by breaking a window large enough to allow him to crawl in with room to spare. He then proceeded to rob the place. He had located a place nearby the window where his *bakfiets* would be nicely concealed. A *bakfiets* is a heavy duty bicycle with a large basket in the front, as well as one in the back. In those days, the *bakfiets* was commonly used for deliveries for small businesses.

He went back and forth through the broken window for as much rice and tea as his two baskets would hold. He then took off like a shot in the dark. We were all afraid to think of what would have happened to him if he had been caught. Punishment was very severe for stealing.

Now, as he shook me awake, I blinked hard, ready to hear what he had to say this morning. I could tell by his excited face that he was up to something possibly dangerous. "Sis," he said while shaking my arm. "You've got to help me."

"Help you?" I asked in surprise. I'd been unaware he was even here at the house today.

"I brought Mother some potatoes for your supper," he said. "But, she has no coal to cook them with."

"Well," I complained. "Why did you have to wake me to tell me a dumb thing like that? I already know that." Brothers could be so stupid.

"Do you want an extra portion of potatoes tonight or not?" he asked impatiently.

That interested me. "What do you have in mind, Bobbie?"

"Don't tell Mother. Promise?"

"Well, what don't you want me to tell her?" I asked, trying to get an answer out of him.

"Promise?" he insisted.

"Oh, you know I won't tell if you don't want me to."

He looked at me as if he needed to convince himself I was really fully awake.

I was growing impatient. "Are you going to tell me or not? If you are just going to stare at me, you might as well get out of my room."

His eyes grew slanted; an expression I knew well. He was very serious about what he had planned. "Remember where the Germans keep their coal storage in that little inlet where they repair their trucks?"

I knew very well the area he was describing to me, but could it be he had forgotten about the large iron-gate separating the garage from the street? The iron-gate had always been a challenge for every child in the neighborhood to climb. The inlet with its coveted coal he was talking about could be reached by connection of an alley-type walkway right behind the iron-gate.

"Oh, Bobbie! We've lived her for eight years. Of course, I know where it is."

"Whoa," he said. "You are a grump today."

I pushed him in disgust.

"If you'd come with me to get Mother some coal, then we can get her two bags. If I go by myself, one is all I'd be able to handle. It's impossible climbing over the gate with two bags."

Bobbie must have noticed the disbelief in my eyes as I thought this through.

"What's wrong with you, Sissie?" he asked. "Are you a German lover?"

"Hey!"

"If you wait by the gate, then I'll go over with my bag. Once I'm over, you climb on the first crossbar of the gate, allowing you to throw your bag over the gate. We'll put the coal in potato sacks. They are big enough, giving us enough room to tie the tops. What do you think, Sissie?"

The idea nearly scared me to death, but an extra helping of potatoes eliminated all the fear I had at the moment. "Do you want to go now?"

"Yes," he answered. "That is if you want to eat your potatoes cooked."

Without any more hesitation, I got up to walk to the corner closet to pull my coat off the wooden hanger. Then, doubt set in again. "Are you sure it will be all right, Bobbie?"

"Of course," he replied. "It's almost dark. They're working inside repairing their trucks. They're not going to be outside when it's cold like this."

That made good sense after he told me that.

It wasn't difficult slipping out of the house unnoticed. The cold hit us once we stepped outside. Neither was it going to be a hard climb reaching the other side of the gate. After all, we'd had plenty of practice. The alley leading up to the inlet was about fifty meters from the gate. I visualized the area with the huge mountain of black coal in the northwest corner, but then, I also remembered the large wooden garage door on the side of it. What was behind that door? The enemy!

"Oh, Bobbie," I said again. "Are you sure?"

"Since when have you turned chicken, Sis?" He knew talking like that, he could make me do anything.

I finished buttoning up my coat. Bobbie handed me one of the gunny sacks and warned me not to fill it too full once we got to the point of destination. "You want to be able to run with it," he instructed.

Bobbie grabbed me by the hand sensing my reoccurring hesitation. "Come on, Sis," he urged, "They'll all be inside where it's warm," he repeated once more. "Nothing is going to happen."

Our street was totally deserted. It was only moments after we left home that we arrived at the gate.

"You're right," I said with a sigh of relief. "The Germans are all in the garage."

Bobbie didn't hear me. He was too busy scanning the area. "Okay, Sis. It's safe. Start climbing."

"Will you be right behind me?"

When he didn't answer, I could feel my throat tighten as the moment was here.

"Hurry, start climbing," he urged impatiently. "Get over that gate!"

I did as directed, reaching the top in no time at all, being careful not to get caught on the steel spokes on top of the gate, being careful not to drop the potato bag.

"Good girl," Bobbie said with approval as he watched me go down on the other side. It was his turn to start climbing. I watched him in amazement as he practically flew up and over and then down the gate.

"Stay on the side of the building; don't move until I say for you to."

He moved up to the inlet in a half-walk, half-run, while staying close to the wall. He turned and motioned for me to follow him. I reached the inlet, watching with relief that no one was in sight, only the object—a huge heap of coal.

"Bobbie!" I nearly screamed his name. "We didn't bring a scoop to get them up with."

"Use your hands, Sis," he said in a matter-of-fact voice. "Be quiet above all else. Someone could hear us."

Bobbie opened his bag and started scooping up the coals with his bare hands. He worked fast without stopping until the bag was filled in no time with the amount of coal he'd be able to handle going back up the gate.

"Hurry, Sis. What's the matter with you? Scoop by the handfuls, not one by one." He bit his bottom lip in disgust. "We'll be here all day. Oh, here let me do it."

I moved over to let him finish. "I'm sorry. It's just that they are so dirty."

"Girls," he said with a groan as he started to fill my bag.

I kept a close eye out for any sign of life while holding the bag. So far, it had been a successful robbery.

"That's enough," I said nervously.

"Just a little more," he said. "Can you carry this much?"

"Yes, yes. Let's go, okay?"

"Tie the knot as I showed you."

My hands felt like clumps of ice making it difficult trying to tie the rough material of the potato sacks into a knot. As I managed it, I heard a window open in an apartment dwelling opposite from where the garage was located. Bobbie heard it at the same time. We both glanced up to see who would be opening their window on this bitterly cold evening. We watched and listened in horror as a woman in the window started to holler at us.

"What's she saying, Bobbie?" I asked as I got more and more scared by the minute.

"That stupid old biddy says she's going to tell the Germans on us for stealing."

"Oh," I whispered, "Why doesn't she stop?"

"Come, Sis. We've got to get out of here before the Germans hear her."

He grabbed both bags and started running toward the gate with me following on his heels. As we reached the gate, we both heard the garage door opening, followed by dogs barking. Even with all the other distractions, we could still hear the screeching voice of our betrayer giving the Germans information on what was going on.

Bobbie frantically started his climb up the iron-gate tugging and pulling his bag of coal along with him. Poor Bobbie. He had filled his bag much more than he had mine making it a heavier burden. Following instructions, I waited at the bottom of the gate until he arrived at the top. Then, I was to stand on the first crossbar, reaching the bag up to him.

We could still hear the old biddy screeching away, trying to make the soldiers understand what happened. It was a stroke of luck she couldn't converse with them in their own language, thus allowing us a few extra precious moments for our getaway. To my horror, I watched Bobbie jump down from the gate and disappear around the corner.

"Bobbie!" I shouted out at him. "Wait for me!" My knees felt weak and tears were swelling up in my eyes. "Bobbie!" I screamed once again.

I could hear the dogs bark excitedly as the soldiers tried to contain them on their leash. My decision was quickly made. I dropped my bag of coal and then scurried up the gate, making it to the top in a split second. However, in my haste to clear the top to start my journey down the gate, I had forgotten to avoid the spokes. As I swung my legs over, my dress got twisted on the iron. I yanked hard and could feel it tear right before it gave away to my weight pulling at it. At any moment, the soldiers were bound to appear around the corner. By now, I was crying hysterically.

Halfway down the gate, the first soldier appeared.

"Halt!" he shouted.

I saw him raise his gun and a shot went off. The frightening sound of that explosion was followed by my frantic scream. I fell to the street below, landing hard on the cement. No pain was felt at that moment of fear and panic. Only frantic thoughts ran through my head as I scrambled up off my scuffed knees. I looked up to see the soldiers making it halfway down the alley. Doubt of whether he was going to shoot again, added more dread to my thoughts. The dogs were still barking furiously.

Hide, hide, run, run!

Oh, how I did run!

I also knew where to hide.

Run!

Instinct told me there wouldn't be time to make it all the way home. By the time Mama would answer the door, the soldiers and dogs would have caught up with me. There was a porch nearby that had a deep, cubby hole, one of my favorite places to hide when my buddy, Hank, and I played hide and seek. My legs were moving me fast in that direction. I ran up the steps leading up into the hiding place, away from frightful barking dogs and the fearful screeching of the old lady. I felt safe at last, if only for a moment, for I could still hear the dogs snarling. The soldiers had unlocked the gate, pursuing their search.

Panic seized me. The dogs could find me even though the soldiers might not. I heard them go past the steps leading up to the hiding place. All of a sudden, I heard Mama's voice in my mind saying in her comforting words, "If you ever become very, frightened, you must say a prayer and help will come."

My prayer was short, but mighty. It was a simple prayer of a child, I don't remember what I said, but it worked. I knew the only way to avoid being shot dead was to ask the only person who could prevent this from happening. Even though the sounds of boots and dogs grew faint, it would be best to wait a long time before I tried to go home.

The cold was numbing my hands and feet. My dress was hopelessly torn and my face felt gritty as I wiped away my tears with coal-covered hands, I knew must be leaving traces of black streaks on my face.

Thoughts of Bobbie abandoning me stuck on the gate with the soldiers and their dogs right on my heels infuriated me all over again.

I'll never talk to him again, I promised myself. *Worse yet, I'm going to tell Mama and Papa everything. I don't care if I get in trouble.*

All these wonderful thoughts of revenge made time waiting in my hiding place go by quickly. It was dark at last. Mama would be worried, but hopefully Bobbie made it home. When I decided it would now be safe to go down the steps, I took them slowly, step-by-step, preparing to scurry back to the hiding place at any suspicious sound. My legs didn't want to move, not only because of the anxiety of the last few moments, but also because of the bitter cold. I grabbed the railing to support me. Halfway down the steps, I could feel the chilling wind reaching me from the street below.

Did Bobbie make it home?

My nose felt frozen. How could I make it stop running? I was confronted with a thousand problems, but none as important as finding the courage to enter the street below. The dark of night, the unforgiving wind, and hunger and fear combined with a fierce determination to get home made up my mind to start running.

Looking neither to the left nor right, and having the sight of my home to spur me on, I reached the front door swiftly. It only took one knock when the entry flew open and the sight of Bobbie's grinning face welcomed me.

As mad as I had been with him, I was relieved to see him and to know that we were both safe.

"Where have you been, Sis?" he asked curiously and with a wink.

There was no time for answers. I leaped into his arms and tears started to flow.

"Oh, Sissie," he said tenderly. "Forgive me for leaving you. If the soldiers had caught me, they would have shipped me off to Germany to work in their factories in a second."

I nodded in understanding while I held tightly.

"I had to count on you to climb over that gate fast enough to get away in time."

Not listening, I sobbed. "Oh, Bobbie, they shot at me."

"I know, Sissie. I heard it," he said sympathetically. "You can't imagine how badly I wanted to turn back to help you, but I couldn't. I thought even the meanest of them wouldn't purposely shoot a little girl in cold blood. I kept running until I reached the house." He held onto me until my sobbing stopped.

"Where's Mother? Does she know?" I asked.

"No, nothing. She's giving baby Nola a bath in the kitchen."

"Is Father here?"

"He hasn't come home from the office yet. Hurry and get your face washed," he said to me. Then, he added, "You look like you fell in a coal bin, face down.

We both laughed at this silly statement. He gave me the once over very carefully and noticed my dress in shambles.

"What happened?" he asked in surprise.

"Oh, one of the spokes on top of the gate got me and tore my dress, too."

He laughed at my tone of voice. "Never mind. Give me your coat first and then take off your dress. I'll get your nightgown. We'll tell Mother you don't feel well, but for goodness sake, wash your face and hands first."

He hurried me into the washroom. Even though the water was icy cold, it felt warm against my frigid hands and face. Bobbie brought me my nightgown which was hastily exchanged for my torn dress. I snuggled up grateful in the overstuffed chair in the front room, tucking a blanket tightly around me.

"Warmed up yet?" Bobbie asked as he sat opposite me.

"Mama doesn't know, right?"

"Not a thing."

"How did you keep it from her?"

"I told her the Merle's gave the coal to us."

"What did she say?"

"Nothing," he said as he shrugged his shoulders. "She said, 'How nice.'"

"What if she thanks them and they don't know what she's talking about?"

"Don't worry, Sissie. I'll take care of it."

His answer satisfied me. He meant what he said and I knew he would keep his word. Bobbie was a great brother. He possessed the wisdom of an eighty-year-old man.

"Were you scared, Sis?"

"Oh, yes. It was awful!"

Bobbie noticed tears coming to the surface once more. "Don't cry now—it's all over."

"You know where I hid?"

"Where?"

"The cubby hole where we always played hide-and-go-seek."

"Good one," he said and laughed.

While thinking back on our experience of that late afternoon, I suddenly remembered the fate of my contraband. My expression must have given it away for it was as if my brother had read my mind when he said, "I guess you left your bag of coal behind, huh?"

When I started to apologize, he held up his hand. "There's enough here for a long time. I really filled my bag full."

Just then, Mama opened the kitchen door. A gush of warm air followed her into the living room together with a sweet aroma of potatoes cooking. I peered over at my dear brother's smiling face. I could forgive him at the moment for anything he had ever done to me. We had reason to be very proud of ourselves and our accomplishments that day.

"Hopie!" Mother said, calling me by my pet name, "Your visit with the Merle's was rather lengthy today, wasn't it?" she asked sternly.

I felt uneasy about not being able to tell her the truth. It would take a ton of explaining on my part if Mother ever found out there had not been a visit to my best buddy's parents' house.

Bobbie's foot touched mine gently in reminder not to answer her question.

"Oh, yes! Sorry."

"Make sure you are home before dark from now on. Remember that, Hopie. Okay?"

"Yes, I promise." I took the baby from her arms. How sweet she smelled. Her soft, damp hair tickled my face as I held her close. How happy I felt that this sweet bundle didn't have to be afraid of anything. My mind switched from Nola to the delicious aroma of food cooking. "Mama," I asked, "When are we going to eat?"

***

I remember another occasion when Bobbie was the cause of freaking out my mother. Once again, my brave brother, together with some of his comrades, had chopped down a telephone pole. Can you imagine the punishment for that? He came to the front door with this dirty, long pole and brought the thing into our house.

Poor Mother must have thought, "Oh, we are dead for sure."

No... but we did have fire wood for a long time.

***

Looking back, it seems to me as if Bobbie's sole purpose in life was to freak our mother out.

We refer to the following incident as the "Fish Story."

It was an ordinary winter's day, as regular as one could hope for. That afternoon, when all her housework was finished and her two youngest children went down for their naps, Mother was surprised with a visit from Bobbie who arrived on his bike. With the fear of one's bike being stolen, it became good sense to park anything of value inside the house, which he did.

Once again, our father had provided a falsified pass for Bobbie, permitting him to keep his bike during the war years. He told Mother he was on his way to deliver some fresh fish to one of his mother's black market customers. We all knew his mother had a lucrative business on the side.

Bobbie's visits were always much enjoyed by his younger siblings. To us, he was the famous Robin Hood of long ago revamped in the twentieth century. Entertaining he was! As heartless as it may have seemed at the time, when he left me stranded on the top of the garage gate while running away from the German soldiers carrying his bounty of stolen coal, I had long since forgiven him. But, what happened next gave me a delicious sense of satisfaction.

The smell of the fresh fish strapped onto the back of his bike had been ignored by all of us, but not by our cat, Hummus. Since she also suffered much with an empty belly, she had given the fish all of her attention. Poor Bobbie! When he said his good-byes and was ready to go on his way, all that was left of the black market fish were some bare bones and a smelly wrapper.

"How am I going to explain this?" he wailed.

My unconcerned mother said sarcastically, "Just tell the truth."

Our friend, Han.

Chapter Eleven

HAN

Days dragged on with more hardships staring us in the face. Fuel, there was none. In desperation, to stay warm in their homes, it wasn't at all uncommon for the Amsterdammers to tear wooden doors off their hinges and use it for firewood. Many rooms in homes ended up doorless with the contents soon disappearing into the wood-burning stove.

Hunger was felt everywhere. The bread lines were longer than ever before. Supplies normally arriving by train, from the country side, were frequently bombed by the Allies because the German Army transported their weaponry and other war supplies by train from one destination to another. The Allies' bombers had no knowledge of which trains carried food supplies into the cities.

In spite of the scarcity of food, Father added a new member to our family. His name was Han Hamel. Han was by no means a stranger to us. His widowed mother and two sisters were well-loved and revered, not only by our family, but by every member of the Haarlem L.D.S. branch of which they were members.

On one occasion, when the trains were still running, Father had taken me along with him to one of the church meetings he had to conduct. After the evening church service, the two of us were invited to stop by Han's house.

Han's family had a lovely home which made a lasting impression on me. As my memory of this place would have it, we had to enter through a rather large iron gate. The stone wall surrounding the dwelling was covered with climbing vines, giving the entrance way a Gothic impression. The courtyard was rather large by Dutch standards. Our tiny country had no land to spare for all of Holland is only 17,000 square miles. A wonderful, large willow tree added even more charm to Han's quaint dwelling.

The pathway to Han Hamel's home led to a big, wood-carved door adorned with a huge lion head door knocker. On both sides of the cobbled walkway, there were rows of lovely rosebushes which Haarlem was well-known for. Haarlem with its wonderful history, its grand architecture, the old city wall (part of it is still intact) including the Old City Gate, dated back almost eight centuries only to be outdone by the Capital of Holland, the beautiful old city of Amsterdam.

Father allowed me to make our visit known by setting the lion head in motion. Once inside, I took in all the splendor around me. The front foyer was spacious, which was very likely a duplicate of an old master's painting. An antique grandfather clock added even more charm to this cozy entrance. French doors led us into the living quarters. A huge, colorful glass and lead Tiffany window adorned the east wall of the front room.

As the sun was setting, rays of sunshine penetrated through the window. The room was ablaze with a huge swath of color. It took the appearance of a rainbow which had been shattered into a million pieces. This panorama of color fluttered through the room much like a huge swarm of beautiful butterflies, clinging to the wall and ceiling.

Sister Hamel smiled as she noticed our reaction. "This is the first time you've come to visit us?"

Still too stunned by all of this beauty, I simply nodded my head with a, "Yeah, first time." Then, I tugged my father's hand. "Papa," I whispered, "Is Heaven going to be this beautiful?"

I could tell Father was pleased with me when I asked this question because he broke out into a hardy laugh.

Some months later, Sister Hamel asked if Han could stay with us for a while. She explained that her son was to be questioned by the Gestapo. The place and time had been set for the appointment.

The four of us children were absolutely delighted with Han's company. Tall and lanky, with a big smile set in a sweet, handsome face, this twenty-year-old could work his way into anyone's heart. He possessed a mystical power allowing him to look beyond the curtain of reality. There, in his mind, he had created for us an imaginary world of beauty and innocence. He was a wonderful story teller. There is so much of Han I have forgotten except for his wonderful stories. Han made Mother Goose come alive. Han made us cry when the wicked step-sisters made Cinderella work so hard. Han made us laugh with joy when the prince slipped the glass shoe on her foot.

Many hours were spent with our new beloved Pied Piper as he would draw us into this wonderful imaginary world of his. In reluctance to leave this self-created sanctuary—his wonderful stories had carved themselves deeply into our minds—carefully nurtured, then placed into an everlasting memory.

In time, it became a struggle for our friend from the Haarlem Branch to adjust himself in our cramped quarters. His stories became less frequent and our English lessons cancelled. Ultimately, his demeanor had become quiet and somewhat sad.

One evening, after curfew, he simply said, "Sister Betty, I need to go for a walk. Please don't stop me."

Nevertheless, Mother pleaded with him not to go. "Wait for John to get home," she urged. "He'll think of a way for you to get out of the house for a while without placing yourself in danger of being caught by the Germans."

Han simply left, never to be seen again. We feared Han had become another of the occupiers' many victims. The disappearance of Han affected the family deeply. Father blamed the "after curfew pass" he had given him. Had it been questioned? Had there been suspicion that it was a falsified document? Many sleepless nights were spent pacing the floor.

Ada's father, John.

Chapter Twelve

THE CHIMNEY

The place was sparsely furnished with whatever second-hand furniture the group could muster up. Mr. Oskam, Father's right hand man, generally called "Mr. O.," lucked out at an auction where he purchased some crudely built bunk beds along with an antique table. The table took up most of the small office, leaving little space for the printing press and beds. The third member of the group, Mr. Franken, was often caught mumbling some choice words when he'd bump into the sharp corners.

Mr. Franken tried to stay optimistic through this cramped situation, yet he still ended up with the nickname "Grumpy." Fortunately, for the three of them, a large men's room with shower facilities was located directly across the hall from the basement room. It had a small, oblong window facing the unused back lot of the building. Huge climbing vines covered the wall and the window creating a perfect cover for their operation.

Cleaning the dirty facility after it had been sitting vacant for at least a decade proved to be a horrendous job. The end result was a super clean bathroom. Their overnight stays in the basement had become tolerable.

Over breakfast at home one day, Father told us what had happened the previous day at the office. He and Mr. O arrived that night and sat chatting and kidding about how wonderful it would be to have a proper meal again, like a steak as big as a house and a truckload of potatoes. While they waited for Mr. Franken to arrive, Father decided to get rid of old bulletins by burning them in the boiler room oven located on the same floor of their working place. The building's janitor had joined the resistance group and for some time had been faithful to do everything it took to keep the secret room from being discovered by others working there. The location of the boiler room had been enormously convenient for disposing of all the excess materials that may have connected them with their underground work.

Father said, when Mr. O opened the door of this huge oven, a gush of hot air overwhelmed both of them.

"It must have been very windy outside," Father said, as he recalled what happened. Mr. O told him it was indeed cold and wet and windy outside.

Another draft of air came, creating a whirlwind that scattered the news bulletins in every direction inside the fiery furnace. They quickly shut the door. The fire inside created a spooky atmosphere in the room with flames creating huge shadows on the surrounding walls.

Father smiled and said, "Mr. O said he had 'the frights.'"

The two friends went back to their secret room and waited for Mr. Franken.

Father said he was relieved the extra bulletins were now destroyed. Back in the secret room, the two men were enjoying a few quiet moments, but were suddenly interrupted when Mr. Franken burst in. Father said his red hair and face were drenched with perspiration.

He told them, "The bulletins are all over the street outside the building."

The two other men looked at Mr. Franken in disbelief.

They told him it wasn't possible because they had burned them all in the furnace.

Mr. Franken threw his hands up in desperation repeating that the bulletins were all over the street and if they did not believe him, they should go outside and look.

Once outside, they saw their friend was not kidding.

"It must have been the wind outside causing a draft in the furnace and sucking the bulletins up through the chimney," Father told us.

They were scared being outside because it was already curfew. When they entered the courtyard, bracing themselves against the cold, dark evening, they ran across to the guard house. The dimly lit building showed no sign of life and the gate was open. Without a star in the sky, it was difficult to detect anything or anybody in the thickness of the dark. The wind had died down and the heavy downpour had changed into a light drizzle.

Father said, "We nearly panicked when we saw a shadow of a person at the entrance of the open gate, but then recognized it to be our friend, the guard."

The guard told them to get going and gather the papers. "If it wasn't for the rain making the papers stick to the ground, they would have blown away."

Fortunately, the Germans were not fond of our rainy weather, so that was probably why there hadn't been any of them on the street.

The guard told them, "I could not believe my eyes when I saw the chimney spewing out a big white cloud of paper material."

After the rain-soaked papers were gathered, it was decided it would be too dangerous going any further than the surrounding area of the office building. Father said they believed if there were any papers left, the ink would have been washed off. With most of the papers secured, they hurried back into the main building, leaving the guard to close the gate.

"I certainly appreciate my friends more than ever after all that happened," Father said. He had the utmost respect for his two special friends, and, with his voice full of emotion, he said, "I told them they might not be religious, but what the three of us experienced must have convinced them there is a God in Heaven looking out for his mortal children."

These three dedicated men, serving God and country, bowed their heads that night with Mr. O and Mr. Franken joining Father in silent prayer.

***

After much thought about how to make the falsified documents more credible, Father and his comrades decided a Nazi stamp was needed. So, Father's plans were made to steal one.

"Steal a stamp? No, John, this can't be done. It's too dangerous!" Mother pleaded. Her reaction to his daredevil tactics were mingled with fear and anger.

"Urgent times, urgent needs," was Father's response.

It would take a mountain of reassuring before Mother felt at least somewhat at ease with their plan. "What if you are caught stealing the stamp? Then what?"

"All right, Mama. Let me again explain what is to be done so you will understand completely the importance of this undertaking." When he managed to calm her down, he seated himself in front of her and, holding her hand in his, he went on. "Now, listen good and don't interrupt. I know you are scared, but believe me, this is going to work for us."

With Father's explanation of why it was so important to obtain the stamp, Mother was convinced. It took much planning for the members of the resistance group as to how this heist was to be carried out. Strategies were made in the basement area of Father's place of employment. When an additional wing on the west side of his office had been added, the basement areas that had once been used as part of the other offices—which were abandoned decades ago—were only now to be used to store old files. The presence of these former offices had long been forgotten by most of the employees of the Amsterdam Utility Company.

As for now, it made a useful place for the resistance workers. The printing press, the radios, and everything else needed to carry on the work had been well-hidden and was out of view. The office building itself was located on a quiet side street off a busy main road in Centrum, Amsterdam.

Tall, old, and decayed oak trees stood quite stately on opposite sides of the street hiding the office building in its shadows. Like so many of the older structures in the Old City, it also had a guarded gate. Before the outbreak of World War II, the guard house stood unused. However, since then, the Germans had taken over the top floor of the building for administration purposes. The guard house was now in full use. Passes were issued to the employees to leave or enter the building, a slap in the face for every Hollander who worked there, but not one person dared to comment on this in the open.

After everyone had done their complaining about this awkward situation, working beside the enemy in one place, proved ultimately to be helpful in the future for the resistance group. Following considerable debating of a safe way to obtain the much-needed Nazi stamp to finalize falsified documents, the group decided on the German occupied third floor in their building, whose office supplied the needed stamp. Unknown to the Germans, Father possessed a master key to all the different offices. Surely, this was a lucky oversight for the group. So, now that the *where* had been established, the *when* had to be decided.

A meeting had been scheduled after the three men, Mr. O, Franken, and my dad, got word to gather in their secret room. Plans needed to be made on how and where to steal the Nazi stamp. They seated themselves around the table in deep thought, entering the room after Father. Meanwhile, Father scoured up some bundles of outdated files to start a cozy fire in a small wood burning stove that had been abandoned many years ago. Luckily, it was still in good working order. It created a bit of a smell once in a while, but nevertheless it kept them warm in the somewhat chilly evenings. Their secret room, through months of utilizing it, had taken on a "just like home" appearance. The three men had brought an item or two to spruce it up a little. Mr. O had even contributed a large rug for the cement floor, "just to keep our feet a little warmer" he said with a grin.

Father now interrupted the long silence between the two men and asked, while poking rather furiously into the now crackling fire with a long black poker, "How long has it been since the Nazis occupied the upper floor?"

Mr. O looked puzzled at the question. He turned to Franken expecting an answer from him.

"About a year," Franken answered.

"Good guess. That's what I thought," agreed Father. "So, we know pretty well about their comings and goings, right?"

"We have definitely given this much of our attention," Franken said.

Mr. O joined in, "Oh, ya, who could possibly not notice their Saturday night drinking binges?"

"No way, John," muttered Franken, who had obviously figured out where this conversation was heading and what Father was hinting at.

With that, Mr. O gave Franken a good kick in the shins under the table. "Let him talk," he said impatiently. "Go on, John" encouraged Mr. O. "I believe by now we both know what your plans are and I'm in."

With that kind of support, Mr. O was rewarded with a grateful smile from Father.

Father continued. "Now that you know what this meeting is all about, let me assure you what I am about to share with you will be the only way we will be able to get our hands on a Nazi stamp." His lips tightened as he prepared how to present the daring plan to them.

Franken was a cautious man and Father knew it was going to be difficult convincing him. Mr. O was, or so it seemed, already convinced that whatever Father came up with, was okay with him. His trust in his friend had never been challenged. The two men, now all ears, sat and listened for Father to go on.

"We just mentioned the soldiers' beer parties. Well, that is exactly what we are going to take advantage of. The heist is going to happen when the Nazis are upstairs with their girlfriends having one of their get-togethers. The guard at the gate will be included in this. I've already spoken to him and he has agreed to do all he can to make this a success."

"He's a good man," said Franken. "He's always been dependable."

"During one of these parties is a perfect time for the heist to happen, isn't it? When they are having their fun up there," Father said.

"Couldn't be better timing, perfect," agreed Franken.

"Glad you are with us, Franken," said Mr. O. "We need you. What about the girls who generally join them?" Mr. O went on.

"They'll be there all right. Have they ever missed coming?" Father asked. "The girls will come right after dark."

"Those wenches!" Franken said in disgust.

"That may be true, Franken, but right now we need those women to distract the soldiers. In the past," Father continued, "before the drinking started, they played music. We also know soon after the socializing, the drinking starts and soon they will all be intoxicated. That's when I go into action finding the stamp we need."

"Did the guard indicate to you how many soldiers were left upstairs partying after the others went back to their places?"

"Well, yes. That's a good question, Grumpy," said Father. "Sorry, Franken, but goodness knows you deserve that nickname."

"Yes, yes I suppose so." Then, a good natured slap on the back coming from Mr. O pulled up a grin on Grumpy's face.

Father loved these good men. Folks like these were worth fighting for.

He continued with the plan. "We know the guard has free roam of the building. He agreed that he'd give us a sign when the drinking has gone on a while."

"John," Franken interrupted again. "Sorry, but where does the drinking take place? In their offices?"

"We have always assumed how many German soldiers work on the upper floor, luckily the guard knows, for he made it a point to count the ones who leave and the ones who stay to party. They party in the conference room upstairs. You have a question, Mr. O? You are starting to look uncomfortable."

"No, no, it's just hot in here. There is something though. You have a pass key to all the different offices, are you going to need these keys?"

"Oh, yes. Their offices will be locked by them as they leave to party in the conference room. Strict orders."

"So, the guard doesn't have the keys?"

"No, I was given the pass keys when I was promoted to my current position. I don't believe anyone knows I even have them except for the two of you. I don't know exactly which office would have a stamp on their desk, but I assume they'll all have one."

"How many offices are in use up there, John?"

"Just three."

Mr. O furrowed his brows. "After you get the stamp, will you duplicate it down here?"

"Yes, Mr. O, down here. We will have everything we need in place here. It will have to be done quickly so I can put it back after I have borrowed it."

All three men bust out in laughter when the term "borrowed" was used.

"Are you still with me, guys?" asked Father.

The answer came quick and with certainty, "Yes!"

"Just one more thing, John," noted Franken. "Will the girls present a problem?"

"I doubt it. According to the guard, these are party girls and do their part drinking, as well. Besides, they will be in the conference room. The offices are off limits to them."

"You almost make this sound easy, John," Mr. O said with a smile.

"Where do we come in?" Franken asked with an uneasy tone of voice.

Father nodded at them. "Before I answer, there is something I need to explain. We will have some outside help. A good, trusted man from another resistance group we are affiliated with is going to meet us here next Saturday. This man will help us with the duplication of the stamp and he will have everything we need with him to do the job."

"*Can* he be trusted?" asked suspicious Mr. O.

"He can. For he's been active in the resistance for several years now. This man is from Poland, a real patriot, being one of the first to start the underground movement in the Netherlands. He left Poland before his country was invaded by Hitler's armies. I don't know much else about him," Father said. Then, he continued, "Other than that, I know he is a well-known scientist, someone the Germans would very much like to get a hold of."

"What's his name?" asked Mr. O.

"His name hasn't been given out at this point for reasons unknown to me. I know he speaks four languages, German being one of them."

"Seems to me this man was lucky to get out in time," said Franken.

"Lucky for him and lucky for us," said Mr. O. "How did you find him?"

"To tell you the truth" Father said. "He found me. When it was discovered by other groups that the upper floor of our office building had been taken over by the Germans for their administration purposes, he became interested and contacted me. Can't tell you why the interest in the upper floor, perhaps we'll find out later. Anyway, I indicated my desire for a stamp and what my plans were to steal one and he immediately volunteered to help. The Polish man told me he'd been well-trained in the area of falsifying many different documents and passes." Father paused. "Umm, like we do, only on a much bigger scale. The guard has been notified what's going to happen here next Saturday. He will be on duty that evening. The Polish man will use the password to get through the gate."

"What password? His or ours."

"Ours, '*Ik kom van Joop*' will be used by him." That meant "John sent me."

The conversation became tense. The thought of an unknown person taking part in Father's plan seemed risky. He sensed the uneasiness. "Please don't concern yourselves about this man for he's been a member for a long time. In fact, he's been instrumental in helping countless Jews escape across the English Channel into England where they found well-deserved freedom. He's been a member of a huge network of resistance workers in Poland, as well as in this country," Father assured the two men once again.

"Just out of curiosity," asked Franken. "Why did he bother with little old us?"

"Why, Franken, I asked him the same question. Interesting enough, his answer was everything and everyone is important in this work we are all engaged in. If one life is saved, then a whole generation of lives has been saved, also."

"I'd like to meet this guy."

"Well, that time is soon to come," answered Father. "One more thing before we wrap this up. Our Polish friend will come in disguise as a delivery man bringing office supplies as usual. We can't be too careful."

Saturday finally arrived. Mother had included me in Father's plan to heist the stamp. We had been in difficult situations before, but I felt this one seemed to top them all. We reluctantly watched Father leave the house to meet his people in the secret room.

He purposely left the house early that late afternoon so he'd be the first one there. To his surprise, the guard at the gate stopped him to tell him the Polish man, Franken, and Mr. O had already arrived. Following a brief exchange of ideas with the guard at the gate house how this heist of the stamp may play out, Father hurried in the office building where he found the three men waiting for him.

After a short introduction, the four men seated themselves around the wooden table. It gave Father a moment to look the man from Poland over.

Father thought he was a pretty average looking man. He had dark and wavy hair, brown eyes, handsome features, almost a little feminine. Father could not believe this young-looking man was the well-known scientist.

"Sorry," Father spoke in German being somewhat embarrassed having his evaluation of his Polish guests discovered.

"It's all right, you are not the first. I'm used to it," the Polish man said curtly.

Father laughed and wondered what kind of scientist this man was, being able to read his thoughts like that.

The Polish man brought a small suitcase with him which he opened and took the contents out carefully, placing them on the table. There was a rather large amount of wax, matches, and some type of carving tools.

"Certainly looks as if he knows what he's doing," said Mr. O, still sounding a bit suspicious.

"How did it go for him getting through the gate?"

"Not bad at all, John. The guard mentioned the disguise had not been needed. He wasn't noticed and blended right in with the rest of us. Most of the German office workers had already left before we arrived."

"Did you ride a bike here?" Father asked the Polish man.

"Yes, I did."

"Good. These bike passes get around," Father said with a grin.

Our friend was done arranging his materials on the table, took off his coat and cap, and then casually threw them on one of the single beds in the room. "Well," he said just as casually. "Who's the one to steal the stamp?"

My father being the only one to understand the man's prefect German, answered him. "Sir, I guess I am."

The Polish man seemed to become a bit friendlier after the polite answer Father gave him. Father then explained to him (in his rather broken German) what his plans were. The man nodded, apparently approving of what had been explained to him.

"Mr. O, throw some of the old files in the stove, will you, and start a fire? It's getting a little chilly in here."

Mr. O did as Father asked. "Sure. Is this guy all right? Is he really with us?"

"Yes. He's okay. No need to worry."

Just then, there were two knocks of the door. "It's the guard. Open the door, Mr. O"

"The soldiers have all left," the guard said hurriedly. "I counted them as they left."

"How many remain?"

"The same four stayed behind that usually do on Saturday. It is getting close now for the girls to arrive. I'll keep in touch. Oh, by the way, the beer has already been delivered, plus their food, etc."

My father overheard the usual comment out of Franken after the girls were mentioned, "those wenches." It got a good hardy laugh out of the guard.

"Franken, behave yourself. Throw more files on the fire. It's still cold in here."

"Getting nervous, John?"

"That's understandable, Franken. We all are."

The Polish man threw a sympathetic glance in Father and Franken's direction. There wasn't much to discuss at this point. Everything had been well-planned out. It was now a matter of another knock on the door from the guard outside for his okay to go.

"You've got the pass key on you, right?"

My father nodded. "Yes, Mr. O. I've got it right in my pocket and I'm set to go when we hear that knock on the door."

The tenseness in the room had now reached its highest peak. Franken broke the uncomfortable silence and whispered, "We need to tell this brave Polish man we appreciate him."

"I already did," said Father. "He understands."

The knock. It came at last!

Franken rushed to open the door for the guard. He stuck his head around the corner warning us the girls had arrived. Father gave Franken a stern look. "How many?"

"More than usual," the guard said. "A half-dozen or so."

"The wenches must be hungry," Franken whispered to Mr. O.

"You know, Franken, I can call them something worse than that if you'd like."

"Yes, man, be my guest."

"A half-dozen, huh? Well, good enough. They will keep the Krauts plenty busy drinking their heads off."

"Yep," snickered Franken.

"You guys give them time now to get going with their drinking," the guard said. "I will know when the party gets noisy because I can hear them from where I will be."

Father shook his hand. "You are a good man. We appreciate what you do for us and for your loyalty."

"No problem. I'll knock on the door again with two hard knocks when it's time so you will know for sure it's me. I need to get back to my station. After the warning on the door, give them some twenty minutes. After that, they should be partying pretty darn heavy." He looked at his watch shining in the darkened room to see what time it was. "It's almost seven o'clock, so it'll be dark soon. Wait for my knock, two short ones," he said again. "They ordered plenty of beer and liquor. Things will surely work out for the best."

"We are bound to succeed with that kind of ammunition," mused Franken.

The guard left, leaving the four men in nervous anticipation.

The knock finally came. Twice hard and loud.

My father jumped out of his chair. "Okay, I'm set. Have things ready to go for the duplication of the stamp. Remember, time is of the essence. I need to get it back on the desk as soon as possible." This was directed to their Polish comrade.

The man understood. He grabbed my father's hand and shook it furiously.

When Father left, the men had great concern for his safety. All that was heard in their secret room was the ticking of the old wall clock. Sitting at the table, Mr. O. clinched his hands in his lap and Franken seemed as if he was saying a prayer.

Every once in a while, one of the three would glance up to the wall clock or look at each other. The clock seemed to sound louder and louder. TICK, TOCK, TICK, TOCK, it rang, 7:15, 7:30. All eyes focused on the clock with pounding hearts.

"Franken?"

"What Mr. O.?"

"What if he doesn't make it and he gets caught?"

"Come on, Mr. O. They call me Grumpy. Are you trying to take my nickname away from me?"

"Oh, shut up, man. I'm just worried about him."

"Well," responded Grumpy. "Do you think I am having a good time over here?"

Their Polish friend gave them both an irritated glare across the table.

Franken scowled. "Oh, look what you did. You made him mad at us."

"Guess I did, Grumpy."

The clock goes on ticking precious time away.

"Oh, my gosh! I can hear him coming down the stairs," said Franken.

"Shhhh! Keep quiet now. I can hear him."

The door to the secret room opened and a jubilant Father came through it with a Nazi stamp held high in his right hand. "Go to work," he demanded.

Our Polish friend didn't waste a moment. The wax had already been prepared and was ready for the imprint.

Franken and Mr. O were full of questions.

"Were the office doors locked? Did the pass key fit in the lock? Did you run into any of the drunk Nazis?"

"Wait, wait," Father said with a laugh. "One at a time. Oh, man, it was a perfect heist. Those guys were having a great time in the conference room without a worry in the world."

"I need your attention," interrupted our Polish friend. He had been soaking in my Father's happiness and more than likely felt every bit of it himself. "John, listen," he said. "This won't be done tonight, but I will take the imprint with me to finish it and shall have it delivered to the guard by me or one of my co-workers."

"Perfect, perfect, perfect!" My father's enthusiasm bubbled over.

"Sit for a moment and catch your breath," Franken said with a smile.

When the Polish man was finally done with his part of the heist, he handed the original stamp back to my very excited father. The Nazi stamp had been carefully cleaned by removing the waxy residue left behind and it was ready to go back upstairs.

My father disappeared once more, climbing the stairs to the upper floor office where he had stolen the stamp from. The drunken sounds coming from the conference room were even louder than before.

Father said a popular saying came to him at that moment: "Those who laugh last, laugh best. Did you hear that you Nazi son-of-a-guns?" He nearly shouted, very assured that with the turmoil inside the "den of iniquity" he couldn't possibly be heard. "Oh," he went on, "those idiots won't even know we stole their stamp."

Being very assured of himself, he turned the key of the office door and placed the stamp on the desk in its proper place. On the way out, he kicked over a waste paper basked full of trash. "Wish I could do this to a particular part of your body, buddy" he snickered with an evil tone of voice. "I can't believe this kind of luck," he said with more appreciation.

The folks downstairs had been anxiously waiting for Father's return and were once again overjoyed with his great success. Our Polish friend grabbed Father by the shoulders and gave him a big hug.

"Guess that's how they do it in Poland," said a surprised Franken.

"Well done, my friend," he said in perfect German. "These Dutch comrades are a very brave people. Good luck. How do you say this in your language? *Tot Ziens*? Until then?"

The three men thanked this brave hero of the Polish resistance which he gracefully accepted. Mr. O hurried to fetch the coat and cap he'd placed on the bed when he first came in the secret room.

"It's safe for you to leave now. The guard is looking out for you."

"Ya, ya," the Polish man said after trying to understand what Mr. O was saying. The man quickly disappeared into the darkness leaving those he left behind with a feeling of comradery on this important journey they were involved with.

It was time to go. The three men left one-by-one as not to attract any unneeded attention. Father was the last to leave. The guard was acknowledged for his part in their operation.

"You know I'd do anything I can to kick these sons-of--gun back to their own country. You know that, don't you, John?"

"Yes, my friend. I know that very well. Thanks again. You took good care of my bike here and took good care of the others, too. You really kept a close eye on them."

Father loved and respected the sincerity of this good man.

The guard asked, "How's your wife? Her name is Betty, isn't it?"

"Betty it is. Yes, she's fine. I had better get on my way as it's close to curfew time."

"*Tot ziens,*" the guard said closing the gate behind my father.

"Me too," my father hollered back to him.

As he arrived home, Father was welcomed with open arms by a happy family. Mother's worries were over. She was overjoyed to have her family together in one place. We were all entertained that evening listening to Father's exciting story about the incredible success of the heist.

"Mama," he said tenderly, "I do believe we have received one of your miracles today."

"I think so, too."

Ada and her mother. "It's 1942. I'm holding Mother's music book. We were on the way to the train station. Mother had to sing a solo in the Haarlem Branch where Father was the Branch President. The soles of my sandals were made of wood. Mother took some scrap materials and nailed it to the wooden soles. Leather wasn't available at the time and shoes weren't for sale in the stores."

When Ada visited Amsterdam in 1985, she stood in the very spot where her German Soldier friend would sit and eat his lunch.

Chapter Thirteen

SOLDIER DEAR

It was March 1945 and it seemed as though Mother Nature was trying to compensate for the ugliness of the war still raging through Europe by giving us some unusual lovely and early spring days. Especially noticeable were the lilac trees with their heavy purple and white blossoms filling the surroundings with a delicate fragrance that seeped its way into the warm spring air of evening.

On such a spring night, uninterrupted by warning sirens of Allied planes approaching or the ever-present pounding of large artillery disturbing the otherwise quiet nights, a feeling of peace had again returned to our country. These few moments of tranquility were not only appreciated by the people of Holland, but perhaps by the enemy, as well. It was not only Mother Nature's seeming concern about the sufferings of war, but in a special way, this worry was expressed by someone I met that spring.

This well-remembered special person taught me at an early age that no matter what circumstance we may find ourselves in, the goodness in man will prevail.

It was my good fortune to meet such a person when learning the difference about "good and the bad" was important. He taught me it is possible to love our enemies.

It all started on a school day when I met this soldier, my friend. School was within walking distance from home in Amsterdam. In the summertime, I took leisurely fifteen minute walks, but in the cold winter, I would move at a rapid pace, sometimes in a full run depending on how cold it was and the same path would take me four minutes tops. This was one of those leisure walks home from school.

My best friend, Lucie, had been patiently waiting for me outside her schoolroom where we would generally meet. She was athletic, tall for her age, and pretty with a bubbly personality which helped establish her as one of the most popular girls in school. Being her friend was fun. Seldom would I miss the opportunity of walking home with Lucie and today was no exception.

The halls were noisy with students leaving their classrooms on the upper floor. The elementary students on the main level of the two story building had been dismissed a few minutes before the fourth and fifth-grade students upstairs. Lucie and I were both fourth-grade students at the Spiegelschool. Like all the other children, we'd hustle for the exit after Lucie made connection with me at her schoolroom door.

"Race you home," she challenged.

"Why? You always win."

"Oh, come on," she said with a laugh while skipping around me and nearly making me trip over her.

"Where do you get all your energy, Lucie? Does your mother keep you on a straight grasshopper diet?"

She asked, "What do grasshoppers have to do with it?"

"Well, for starters, you could put them all to shame the way you are hopping around."

She noticed the irritation in my voice. "Oh, heck," she said. "We can run another time."

Poor Lucie. I watched her out of the corner of my eye, only to see that I had hurt her feelings. I could tease her endlessly without annoying her, often taking advantage of her good nature. However, today I had gone too far. Even so, it looked as if the race was still on.

"Come on, race you down the steps," I said.

Lucie stared at me in total surprise. Her smile reappeared on her sweet face. "Sure, yes, come on."

We scurried down the wide marble stairs in the school's corridor. Her book bag was pounding wildly on her back while she was literally flying instead of running. Once down the steps, she leaned against the huge oak door of the school. Turning halfway, she watched me finish the race.

She laughed at my unhappy face. "Oh, Adie," she said with a giggle. "I'll bet you'll win the race next time."

"Sure," I said as I growled out at her. "Only if you let me." Nevertheless, I thought she was my friend and I loved her with all my heart.

Arm-in-arm, we walked the side busy street. Trams were passing by as noisily as ever, giving firm warning to their approach. The sun felt warm on our faces. An excitement passed through me at the thought of spring with all its loveliness and fun times—sunny days, playing marbles, hopscotch, and beautiful tulips.

"Lucie, did you know the tulip bulbs have all been eaten by everybody? They are all gone," I said.

Lucie looked at me in disbelief. "Are you serious?"

"Yep," I answered. "You haven't eaten any yet?"

"Yuck, no! Why should I?" she asked in disgust.

"Well, I have," I said with a certain pride. "They are nasty!" The memory of those sweet tasting gritty round critters could still make me shiver.

"Why did you eat the tulips, Adie?"

"Because, silly. We were hungry." Then, I added, "My mother doesn't have money to buy black market food; your mother has."

"Do you still eat them?" she asked curiously.

"Only when we can buy them," I replied, shaking my head hard as if to knock loose the recollection of their nasty taste right out of my memory. "I'd rather eat a worm than eat those things again."

"You are so brave, Adie," Lucie said with a certain twinkle in her eye.

"Yeah, I know," I commented with assurance. I did think of myself as being brave because even the children became more involved at home with Father's war activities. His illegal work in the underground organization had become more intense because of the demand for more news from England. Oh, how I would love to tell Lucie about all the exciting happenings going on at our home at this time.

Oh, yes, I could tell Lucie so many wonderful things, I thought again. Telling her how brave I am was probably all right, but convincing her would be much better.

I turned my head slightly to look at my friend. It would seem so natural to share all these things with her. After all, I knew her secrets. Once again, I was tempted to tell her, at least about how we'd set up the printing blocks to print the news bulletin. Part of my responsibility was to crank the long, old handle to set the press in motion and how much fun it was watching the printed bulletins accumulate one-by-one. If I dared, I would tell her about the time my parents were proud of me when a strange person knocked on our door and asked for an illegal news bulletin without first giving the code: *"Ik kom van Joop,"* which meant "John sent me."

Remembering the instructions that were repeated to us on a daily basis, enforcing the importance of "never trust a stranger asking questions," I simply told the caller at the time that I didn't know what he was talking about. I had been praised and rewarded for remembering Father's strict instructions.

Even though Lucie is not a stranger, it still would be wrong to tell her, I thought, losing my enthusiasm to share my secret life with her. Besides, she didn't seem to believe me when I told her about those tulip bulbs we had for dinner the other day. Then, I supposed it was no use telling her about how our neighbors upstairs ate their cat for dinner a few weeks earlier. With this thought, I found myself feeling bad for Mother all over again. Being the cat lover she was, she cried all day when she was told about the poor animal's demise.

"What have you been thinking about all this time?" Lucie asked curiously.

"I don't know," I answered. "Do you think cats go to heaven, Lucie?"

"Oh, you are funny. Of course, they do."

That answer satisfied me greatly.

We turned the corner; Lucie's house was in view. She lived on one of the lovely canal streets in Amsterdam. De Nassau Kade bearing part of the royal name of Holland's monarchy stood proud next to the wide canal being one of many running through the city and spilling into the main canal, the Amstel, then finding its way into the North Sea. Amsterdam's busy water traffic used to transporting most anything from sugar beets to huge lumps of coal piled on the flat canal barges, lent a picturesque scene to an already beautiful street.

A ferry boarding passengers across the canal kept busy most of the daylight hours. Whenever Lucie and I could spare a *stuivertje* (nickel), we'd take the ride on the ferry just for something fun to do.

The kind proprietor operating the ferry generally didn't mind taking us back over for the same nickel. Entirely operated by man power, with cables on each side of the raft spanning the entire width of the canal, the raft would then be set in motion by turning a wheel manually. The spokes of the wheel would catch the cable, thus pulling the ferry from one side to the other. This must have been a physical job for the ferry changed hands very often.

I felt Lucie shake my arm, taking me out of my daydream. "Hey, are you listening? Pick me up tomorrow and we'll walk to school together. Don't be late, okay?"

I answered rather absentmindedly as my eye caught a glimpse of a figure in the distance appearing to sit on the sidewalk.

"Want to come in for a minute? I'll show you my father's new painting."

The invitation was tempting for I was always made welcome in her home. Besides, the loveliness of Lucie's home never ceased to amaze me. The entry was small with narrow steps leading up to a much larger landing, sporting a beautiful, ornate hall tree. Once one entered through the French doors on the right of the landing, it opened up into a large spacious living quarter. Heavy oak furniture decorated the room and the wooden floors were covered with thick, costly Persian carpets. On every available wall hung Lucie's artistic father's paintings. His works revealed him to be the masterful artist my little friend claimed him to be.

Lucie, still waiting for an answer asked impatiently, "Well, are ya?"

"Oh, no thanks. Not now. See ya later."

Not noticing Lucie's reply, my attention once more gazed at the squatting figure in the distance that came in to focus as I came nearer.

There, sitting on the sidewalk with his back propped against the side of a building, was a German soldier casually eating what appeared to be a sandwich. The sight of this soldier representing himself in such a casual manner was so out of character that it not only brought him to my attention, but the other passersby, as well.

Contrary to my reaction, the others glanced over his way, yet hurried on. My stares seemed to amuse him. Curiosity had me in its power. My legs were unable to carry me any farther. Just standing there staring brought a chuckle out of him. He possessed a quick smile which gave me the impression he could be trusted. He carefully sat down his drinking cup and rested his arms on his pulled up knees. His oil-stained green overalls seemed at least two sizes too big for his slight frame. The front was buttoned half-way revealing a T-shirt flashing the typical camouflage colors of war. His well-fitting cap covered light, curly hair. Fair complexioned and with a twinkle in the almost cerulean blue eyes, he appeared very ordinary, human, and rather handsome in spite of his sloppy appearance.

Waving his hand slightly while it still rested on his knee, he signaled me to come closer. My eyes fell on his half-eaten sandwich. I darted my eyes away afraid he may have noticed me staring at the food. However, I wasn't fast enough and noticed the thick slices of cheese between the two hunks of bread. The sight of this sandwich took my breath away.

He said something in his own language. His voice was kind in accordance with the rest of him. Catching a glimpse of his handsome face as I dared look his way again, assured me, once again, there was nothing to fear. His German being similar to my own language made me understand this stranger and newfound friend wanted me to sit by him. Another stolen glance at his sandwich tempted me to do so.

Hurrying over to him as though the decision wasn't made rapidly enough and the opportunity would be gone forever, got another chuckle of approval out of him.

It felt odd sitting next to a stranger who seemingly had made up his mind to make me his friend. Again, he said something in his own tongue and pointed at the lunch bag.

Could he possibly mean he was willing to share his food with me?

My face flushed with excitement or perhaps the understanding of how unsure I still felt with his generous offer. He handed the bag over to me.

"*Essen* (eat)," he said, followed by a nod of his head.

I understood very well.

Regarding him in disbelief and not expecting this type of kindness from someone we'd been taught to fear, an uncomfortable feeling followed.

I pushed the bag away.

"Ach neine, neine," he softly said. *"Essen, Essen."* His voice was kind, but demanding.

The anticipation of bread and cheese was more than I could refuse. In a useless effort to keep from accepting the bag which he placed in my lap, I eagerly opened it. Not a moment of my excitement went unnoticed by my friend. My grateful eyes met his when the first wonderful bite of his coveted sandwich made its way to my eager mouth.

Caught in his approving smile and the kindness of his soft blue eyes, I felt a bond of trust and appreciation between me and my friend.

My mind had been made up not to tell anyone about what had happened on the way home from school that day. I wanted him to be my friend and protector; responsible for a treasured moment forever locked away in heart and mind.

Keeping this secret friendship all to myself became nearly impossible when, once again, "Soldier Dear" chose to lavish his time and kindness on me.

In a similar situation, as it so happened before, one afternoon while walking home from school, I saw him standing there at the garage front entrance waiting for me.

If it had not been for the vivid memory his kind face had impressed on me, I may not have recognized him for he stood there in full uniform.

"Oh, must he look like all the others." I thought frantically. Putting feelings aside, I ran over to him as he had been waving me on to do so.

"Kommen sie." He repeated. *"Kommen sie* (come on)."

On his invitation, I nestled my hand into his rough,

callused one. The uneasiness I felt the first time we met swept over me again. I glanced around, making sure no passerby would notice my hand snuggled in his.

His grip lightened. "*Kom,*" he spoke in German. "We are going to buy a sweet treat, something you haven't had in a long time."

I nodded pretending every word had been understood. I was relieved with the idea I had been one of the last pupils dismissed from school that day because of misbehavior in class. I had been talking instead of listening and now all the other children were well on their way home.

It would have been difficult explaining my friendship with my soldier. Only feelings of hostility were expressed about the enemy in those war days, so how could I make anyone understand that my special friend was different. He returned my smile as I peered up at my handsome escort. We were on our way, but where?

We turned the corner of the canal street across the street from Lucie's house. To my relief, there was no sign of life anywhere around her house. I had kept the secret of my friendship well. Even Lucie, who knew almost all my secrets, had not been included with this one.

I had learned through a scary experience that secrets had to remain tucked away during the time of war. There was a new girl at school. I did so want to give her a good impression of me, so, for a moment, I had forgotten about the many warnings given by Papa never to tell others about the illegal work he and Mama were involved in. One unguarded moment and the secret had been told. Just moments afterwards, I deeply regretted telling her, realizing I might have put Papa and the others in grave danger. A few weeks later, she invited me to her house to see her marble collection. It horrified me when her older sister walked in with her SS officer boyfriend.

The impact of realization of the trust I had broken, betraying my family to my schoolmate, was lived over and over again for many months to follow. It was my good luck that marbles and dolls meant more to my schoolmate than the complexities of war.

Reflecting back to all this brought us to our point of destination. I looked up at the soldier in disbelief when he had stopped by the witch's candy shop.

Is he under the impression the witch is still open for business? I thought.

It had been a long time since she had her pretty candy jars filled with the round, colorful jaw breakers the neighborhood children had loved so much. Since conversation was not possible between my friend and me, facial expressions were somewhat relied on and surely disappointment must have been obvious on my face.

I felt his concern when he knelt down to look eye level at me. In a sympathetic soft voice he said, "*Habe seine angst, ich habe eine uberraschung fur dich.*" (Are you afraid? I have a surprise for you.)

He grabbed the wooden railing for support going down the witch's cellar leading into the small quarters which once was a candy shop. I followed closely behind, sincerely worried about the little old lady the neighborhood children so unmercifully called "the witch" and whether the appearance of German soldier dressed in full uniform would scare her.

He knocked softly on her door and squeezed my hand gently as we stood waiting for some response from inside the cellar. Again, he knocked, only more forcefully than the first.

He frowned, apparently worried about having to disappoint me when again there was no response.

"Maybe we'd better go," I whispered.

He shrugged his shoulders. I felt his impatience. If I could only ask him how he found out about the witch. She had a good business here. I remembered every penny earned by the folks in the neighborhood was readily spent in her shop. Lovely sweets of all kinds including those well-loved, long laces of black licorice she had to offer for merely pennies attracted all those suffering from an incurable sweet tooth. Eventually, her appearance, though frightening, had been accepted by her customers both young and old. She made an awesome impression when dressed in a long, floor-length black gown she generally wore with a black woolen shawl wrapped around her thin shoulders in an attempt to keep the cold cellar draft from chilling her.

I wondered if she still wore her waist-long hair straight with those white shimmering streaks in between the raven black, partly concealing the hump on her back which earned her the name of "witch." No doubt her life had not been an easy one.

After a rather long wait, we finally heard rustling coming from the inside of the cellar. The surprise reaction I had expected never happened when the door slowly opened. She nodded in recognition giving the idea this meeting may have been prearranged. Her eyes darted away from his face to focus on mine. The sight of her still had the same effect on me as it had in the past. Without realizing it, I hid myself halfway behind him in a protective gesture. He put his arm around my shoulder and hugged me close to his side. She gave us a slight smile, partly necessary because of the impressive person in front of her.

"*Kom binnen meneer,*" she said politely in a low voice.

"*Danke,*" he answered.

The once colorful interior of her shop brought on by dozens of jars holding happy surprises had changed into a sad reminder of the present hardships. These same jars now sat empty as though waiting for those joyful days of yesteryear when laughter could once again be heard of excited children anxiously waiting their turn to be helped.

One of the few things remaining of her store was the same old-fashioned register still standing in the same place of the spotless counter top.

After politely inviting us in her shop, she disappeared into an adjacent room which was apparently her small living quarters. The dampness and cold felt familiar, her coal stove in the corner of the shop stood empty and unused as did so many at the time.

She must be very much alone, I thought, with a feeling of regret that I too had made fun of her in the past without a thought of possibly hurting her feelings.

The soldier tapped my shoulder pointing in the direction of the apartment entrance. Carrying a large jar just like the ones left on her shelves, she reentered the shop. It delighted me to see the difference between the jar in her hands and the ones on her shelves. The one she carefully placed on the counter top was full of mouth-watering jaw breakers. Red, blue, green, yellow... they were all there exactly the way I remembered ever so long ago.

The witch seemed untouched by my squeal of excitement. I anxiously watched her every move. My friend gave her little attention. His pleasure was seeing my absolute delight.

She briskly, almost impatiently, turned towards his direction, managing again that same barely noticeable forced smile she managed at her front door.

"*Machen sie den sack voll* (fill the sack)," he demanded.

She understood and filled the pointed bag full of the colorful candies. His grin grew bigger as another squeal of delight came from my direction.

I watched her carefully close the bag, holding it in both hands. It was like a wonderful dream, knowing this sweet treasure would soon be in my possession.

She turned toward him as if she was waiting for the next order to be given. With a slight motion of his head, he indicated to her to pass the candy over to me. She stooped slightly and handed me the bag full of treasures.

"*Dank u wel* (thank you)," I stammered, barely getting the words out. My face felt hot, a funny tickling passed through me, and I could hardly breathe. After taking the bag from her long, skinny hands, I clutched it to my chest with a certain indication that no one in the world could make me part with my bounty. Her eyes were on me, prompting me to look up at her. Expecting an uncaring expression compatible with her mechanical movements and attitude of moments before, I detected glimpses of generosity and understanding. Once again, I felt compassion for this misjudged old woman. The distance that had existed between the two of us, brought on by distrust and prejudice, had been resolved through the kindness of my friend. New understandings had been established.

We left the cellar with one more glance back to give her a smile of gratitude. She paused, returning my smile before quietly closing her door. It was as if I had grown two inches in spirit and mind.

No one knows what happened to her. She seemed to have vanished into thin air, leaving me with a void and a friendship that had never been completed.

My benefactor and I walked back to his garage located around the corner from the candy shop. "*Machstes die meinez lostwagen schn* (Do you want to see my truck)?"

I nodded, trying to imagine what he was trying to tell me. We had arrived at the garage and, judging from the looks we received from the other mechanics, we must have made quite an entrée. Several commands were shouted from different areas of the garage toward "Soldier Dear." I wondered if he was in trouble because of my presence there with him. The smile on his face convinced me all was well.

The garage was huge; much larger in size than I imagined it when passing by it every day to and from school. On the right, inside of the front, stood a small cubical building. It appeared to be the head mechanics office. Scores of trucks were lined up waiting for repairs. Huge overhead electric lamps were burning for the mechanics to work by. Quite the contrast if compared to the small dishes used by Mother that were filled with kerosene oil and topped with wicks to light the room in the evening hours. As my eyes rapidly scanned the rest of the garage taking in all I could of the unusual environment, I noticed daylight pouring in on the far side of the building. The tall doors were both opened wide, exposing a view of a large inlet located outside the open doors.

Clearly in sight was the iron-gate guarding all that was inside of it. All of a sudden, he lifted me off my feet with such a jolt I nearly dropped my bag of candy. Within a split second, I went from garage floor into mid-air, I found myself sitting behind the steering wheel of one of the huge trucks belonging to the soldiers.

I was tingling with excitement spurred on with the smiling faces of the on-looking mechanics. Wouldn't Lucie love this? Sure wish she was here.

Caused by the excitement of the moment, I took a deep breath, filling my lungs, and smelling the combination of oil and gasoline that filled the air. His waiting arms lifted me down out of the truck.

He gave me a quick pat on the behind and said, "*Yehe nach hause mein kleines kind, ich mups seinuck sa-meine arbeit* (You need to go home, little one. I must go to work)."

He stuck out his hand expecting to shake mine. Somehow, I felt a handshake was not enough to compensate this never-forgotten experience of a lifetime. Enthusiastically, I threw my arms around his waist, expressing all the love and respect I felt for my "Soldier Dear." He peered down at me with the same softness in his eyes that made me trust him in the first place. Could it have been for a time we had the opportunity to be friends and I had filled a void in his heart caused by the memory of another ten-year-old girl dear to him, but who was far away from his reach?

The effect of this experience did not linger long for decisions needed to be made. After saying good-bye to my benefactor and waving to his comrades, I hurried on out of the garage. There was still time for a chat with Lucie.

***

Before I had made up my mind, I was going in the direction of her home. Lucie spotted my coming. I watched her move away from the window to open the front door.

"What you got?" she asked with eyes wide with surprise

recognizing the pointed candy bag.

Feeling the need to take a deep breath, I answered, "I'll tell, but not here. Let's go up to your room."

"Yes, yes." There was excitement in her voice.

Once in the house, we both scurried up to the small ladder going into the ceiling opening into Lucie's attic room. I felt safe to tell her about all the wonderful things that had transpired in the last hour. She listened closely; her eyes grew large in disbelief as my story continued on.

"Adie," she interrupted. "You're going to get in trouble."

"Well, not if you keep it a secret."

"How are you going to keep *that* a secret?" she asked pointing to the bag of candy.

"Oh, I'll think of something. Anyway, I can't stand to worry about this now."

She didn't protest anymore after I carefully emptied the bag of candy on her bed. Lucie hand-muffled the excited screech that escaped her.

"Oh, this is too much," she uttered.

Suddenly, she hurried over to my side of the room, placing the candy back in the bag; I hadn't noticed the noise coming from the room below. "Hurry Adie! Under the bed," she said urgently.

Lucie's bed stood on high support, covered with a large, over-sized bedspread. It provided a wonderful hiding place. It had been very useful in the past when Lucie and I would raid her parents' ashtrays, afterwards extracting the tobacco from the cigarette buds. We became very skilled rolling our own in pieces of newspaper. After a few times, we both decided smoking those nasty things underneath the bed and causing us to cough and getting a sick feeling in our stomachs wasn't worth acting grown up.

"Why are we hiding, Lucie?" I asked.

"Because, silly," she whispered, "Would your mother allow you to keep candy given to you by a German?"

The thought hadn't occurred to me. "Of course, she would," I said, remembering I usually got my way with her.

"Well, mine wouldn't. She hates those Nazis." Tucking her arm underneath her while resting her chin in her hand, she asked boldly, "How many are you going to give me?" She already knew, of course, that sharing with her had been part of my plan of what to do with them from the beginning. Keeping my little brothers, Marty and Johnny in mind for their share of my bounty, I handed her four of the colored candies. She seemed happy with her share. She pulled one of her slippers over that had been placed neatly under her bed. The corners of her mouth turned up in total glee after she dropped the candy inside of it.

"Mama will never find them here," she said and giggled.

"I have got to go, Lucie."

"I know. You better hurry."

For one tiny moment, I resented having to share my candy with her. Why, I thought, does she call me that stupid name? Oh well, I guess we are even since she doesn't like the name "Luus" I dubbed her with. We hadn't noticed anymore noises from the room below, indicating it was all right to venture down and then I was on my way home.

It started raining. The sunny sky turned gray and somber, not at an unusual occurrence in our country. It was simply a matter-of-fact. The rainy season had little effect on everyday life.

"Hello, Hopie." Mama said when I arrived home. "Got the laundry off the clothes line in time before it started to rain." She sighed with self-satisfaction, having me wondering if this comment had been directed at me or if she was again talking to herself.

I watched her place the folded sheet carefully underneath the sofa pillows, too busy to notice my drenched condition. "Grandma used to do this, remember? She sure loved that hand-ironed look."

She stopped abruptly, noticing my condition. "Bit wet aren't you, honey? What's in the bag?" By the changing expression on her face, as I was telling her all that had happened the last few hours, I could tell she was not at all pleased. "But, Mama," I pleaded. "He was so nice."

"There is no such thing as a nice German," she snapped. "Give me the bag, Hopie."

"No. No I won't. The candy was given to me."

She reached around me grabbing the bag away from behind my back in my fruitless attempt at trying to hide them out of her sight. The bag tore open in the struggle of possession, scattering the beautiful, colored jawbreakers all over the carpet. With the help of two little brothers, who had been witnessing the whole scene, the candy was quickly picked up off the floor and placed in her apron pockets.

"Mama," I shrieked frantically. "What are you going to do with them?"

"Sorry, Hopie. I will have to get rid of them."

"But why?"

"Hopie," she said firmly. "They could be poisoned."

"No, they are not. They are not, honest. I was right there with Soldier Dear when he bought them from the witch. I told you, remember?"

She gave me one of her stern looks that I so dreaded. "*What* did you call him?"

I repeated his name in a bare whisper. Hearing the term I had given him for the second time only agitated her more. Mama seemed to have made up her mind. She walked briskly toward the back door of her kitchen.

Oh no... she couldn't, I thought, watching her open the patio door onto the veranda. I immediately sensed her next step. To my horror, I watched her lift the lid of the garbage pail and empty her pockets of the jawbreakers. The sound of them hitting the bottom of the empty can would remain with me the rest of my entire life.

She made no apologies this time. She simply went back to her household chores as if nothing had interfered with them in the first place, in spite of my tears. I had lost my chance of retaining my candy by revealing my fondness for my friend. Sharing her children's affections with anyone else, other than herself, let alone with a German soldier, had always been difficult for Mama.

The matters of the day were discussed that night. It was my good fortune Father had a great deal more on his mind than to get involved with the social life of his ten-year-old daughter.

It wasn't mentioned again with the exception of my two little brothers. There was no way of consoling them about this wonderful treasure lost forever.

Row houses in Amsterdam.

Chapter Fourteen

ANOTHER FAREWELL

Many weeks had passed since I'd met Soldier Dear.

I kept a vigilant eye on the garage doors while passing by them on the way home from school in the hopes of once again seeing my good friend. Rain kept the garage doors tightly closed. There was no time to linger anyway. The student body at the Spiegelschool elementary had been instructed by both teachers, as well as parents, to hurry home right after dismissal.

The war efforts had been stepped up by the Allies. Excitement grew among the Dutch people with the happy news of German troops surrendering to the Allies in different parts of occupied Europe. Countless rumors were heard by the young and old. No news seemed too far-fetched. It was all happily accepted. Several families of German soldiers living in our neighborhood were packed and ready to go back to their native Germany. It was a welcome relief, watching these unwanted guests leave.

An overwhelming feeling to celebrate the German defeats existed among the people. However, warnings to be cautious were given for good reason.

The flight pattern of the American and English bomber planes lay directly over the northern part of Holland, which largely included the Amsterdam areas. Although Amsterdam had not been a bombing target as had been other parts of the country, many Allied planes had been shot out of the skies by German artillery, throwing burning debris over the city below and confining most everyone to their homes at night. Danger seemed to always be present. Nevertheless, people were, at this time, preparing themselves for the freedom so longed for.

Just the same, I had not given up keeping an eye out for "Soldier Dear." Even though the garage doors remained closed, hopes of seeing him again never did leave me.

School had been dismissed early the day I was to see him for the last time. After a few weeks of nice, clear skies and sunny days, the weather once again had made a turn for the worse, which made it necessary to utilize the stoker at school to heat the building.

The last of the coal had been used that morning and contained only the smoldering remains. Our early dismissal was welcomed with a loud cheer.

Following the instructions to go straight home, everyone hurried out of the school building. Force of habit prompted me to look for Lucie by the oak doors, but a bad cold had kept her home for several days. I hurried on my way, missing her company. It would have been fun walking in the rain and sharing my umbrella with her. The rain was pouring down. The winds kept tugging hard at the umbrella. Carefully, trying to avoid rain puddles, I still felt water seeping through the soles of both shoes. The card box soles Mama cut out softened the sharpness of gravel, but had little effect with a rainstorm like this one. My shoes were a sight. The toes had already been cut allowing room for my growing feet but, luckily unnoticed by my school playmates. After all, these were times where we all did what we could to keep body and soul together.

I hurried faster, wanting to be home. *How fortunate,* I thought, *that the air raids occurred mostly at night. At least, then we can safely snuggle up underneath the blankets when the very loud sirens were giving their warnings for cover. Oh, my feet are so cold. Next time, I'm going to wear my wooden shoes. I will pay no attention to anyone if they call me* boerin *(farmer's wife). At least, my feet are going to be dry.*

A hundred thoughts helped keep me from noticing my nearly frozen feet. Mother often claimed I had wisdom beyond my years. "You, Hopie," she would say, "will always find a solution for every problem you're confronted with. Now, if you could find a solution to growing so fast, it would be appreciated. At least, until shoe leather is available again."

She's funny, I thought fondly. *Just a few minutes more,* was the thought I prodded myself on with while turning the corner. Our generally busy street was almost deserted. Rain ran down the gutters like wild flowing rivers. The wet pavement seemed like a polished mirror, reflecting all above. I had almost reached the west gate entrance of the garage when I heard the raspy sound of the big, iron gate opening. Afraid to go on, I waited, not knowing what to expect. The eerie sound was quickly followed by the noise of heavy boots coming in my direction. Soon, a German soldier appeared. He gave me a nod of recognition and then a gesture for me to wait. He turned toward the open gate, waving his arm for an all-clear signal, then turned my way again, nodding his head the same way, with the same indication to stay. I heard the sounds of a truck engine starting up filling the afternoon air with a thunderous rumble. A sick feeling came over me, for it became clear to me what all this meant.

Flashing before me, I remembered the German families leaving their homes here to return to their fatherland. Panic gripped my throat and I knew I was about to lose another friend. The first truck approached the gate slowly, making its way through. My suspicions were confirmed when I saw the back filled with uniformed soldiers. I shrieked with terror causing the soldier directing the procedure to look my way.

"*Stephen sie* (stay put)," he spoke kindly, no doubt noticing the anxiety in my face.

The second truck made its way through the gate. I had but a few moments to single out the soldiers on the trucks, one by one. I felt that he had to be one of them. Working my way closer to the gate, I stood next to the soldier.

"You must wait, little girl. He is coming soon," he said in broken Dutch.

"They are moving too fast! I can't see him."

That sick feeling kept churning away at my stomach. One truck followed another in rapid succession. It was almost impossible to identify any one person. Then, while I was holding onto Mama's umbrella, the soldier reached out and tipped the umbrella to one side, making me almost lose my grip of it. I looked in the direction he pointed. My hand muffled the sound of joy escaping from me when I noticed Soldier Dear on the loaded truck. It was but moments later when he saw me standing on the side waving at him. He raised his hand returning the farewell.

For a few seconds, we almost came face-to-face. He exchanged my frantic enthusiasm with one of his kind smiles and shouted something I could not understand. I wanted to run after him, maybe just to tell him I would miss him. He seemed miles away in mere minutes, yet still waving until only a small spot remained in the distance.

Our good-bye had been too quick and I choked back the tears, trying not to cry. The clanging of the gate closing snapped me out of my melancholy thoughts. The soldier in charge of the exodus from the garage to goodness knows where, paused for a moment. He threw a sympathetic glance in my direction. As he turned to leave, the sound of the heels of his boots clicking together, in the manner of the German soldiers, brought me back to reality. With the exception of Soldier Dear, they were the enemy.

Again, I thought of Sonja.

The street was quiet once more. The curtains concealing the curious neighbors who had been witnessing the event on the street below were neatly put in place. That sick feeling I felt before had left me, knowing acceptance was a way of survival in most instances. The need to go home, where kind understanding was to be expected, overwhelmed me even more than my wet, ice-cold feet. All the questions I needed answers for could be found in the secure home down the street.

As soon as I entered our home, I asked Father, "Where could they have taken him?"

"Probably Berlin," Father said with a snare in his voice.

"Berlin?" This comment even made Mother look up from her household chores. Only she knew and understood my friendship with him. She drew me close to her and whispered. "You'll remember him in your prayers tonight and nights to follow, won't you?"

"Yes, Mama. I will."

We had been taught very early in life about the strength of prayer. My mind and heart grew more at ease with this gentle reminder of faith. He may have disappeared out of my life forever on that rainy day, but he would always be, in memory, my Soldier Dear.

A calendar making fun of Hitler during the war.

Chapter Fifteen

VICTORY OVER THE ENEMY

The Allies, after fierce opposition from the enemy on our borders, had at last conquered our county. The Nazi ménage had been wiped out, beaten, and trodden down by the welcoming Allied forces. The comfortable feeling of freedom had infested itself within every living person in our liberated country.

Food arrived from the United States, Sweden, Canada, and other countries, to feed and aid the starving population of the Netherlands. Among the aid and personal encouragement from the United States were items from the Church of Jesus Christ of Latter Day Saints (the Mormons). Much appreciated were the warm and most beautiful homemade quilts made by the Relief Society Sisters. There were shoes, clothing, soap, wheat, cans of Spam, etc. The outpour of love and concern was felt everywhere, coming from all directions.

Our parents, together with the Haarlem Branch, were anxiously waiting for news about Han. We prayed for his safe return. Our hopes were shattered with the disappointing news he had died in a concentration camp.

According to Han's sister, Han had returned to Haarlem, his home town, for a visit and he became ill. His mother and sister took him to the hospital for medical attention. While there, he was immediately arrested for failure to report for duty working in the weapon factories in Germany.

Following his arrest, he was taken to an old freighter along with other prisoners. They were held captive there for many weeks with little food or proper care. Already ill, his health failed him rapidly. When at long last he was taken to the concentration camp, it only took a few months before he passed away.

Our family received the sad news from Han's sister in a letter of appreciation for having hidden him in our home for eight months. "Mother," she mentioned in her letter to my parents, "is much too distraught to write to you, but please accept her heartfelt gratitude."

Han died on February 11, 1945, in the Neuengamme concentration camp within six months after he was arrested. Our much loved friend, Han, has since been sealed in the Latter Day Saint Temple for all eternity. A happy ending for a life well lived with courage and faith.

Translation of Letter from Hans's family

With this note, I would like to thank you on Mother's behalf, and my sister's, for the length of time you provided a hiding place in your home for our Han. After his return home, things seem to be going well for a while, until he was arrested on August 15, 1944.

Just a short time ago, we received the sad news that he had passed away February 11, 1945, in the Neuengamme Concentration Camp. You can imagine how we miss him. Mother is still grieving and taking this very hard. Once more, we thank you for having placed yourselves in a very dangerous situation by hiding Han.

With our most felt gratitude,
Jos Lakerveld

The Dutch flag (red, white, and blue).

Chapter Sixteen

TASTE OF FREEDOM... THE AFTERMATH

The taste of freedom could not have been sweeter when the first Americans, British, and Canadian soldiers marched into their captured territories in Holland. The Dutch flags which had been hidden away for those five years of occupation now openly made their appearance. The Dutch citizens displayed their red, white, and blue even before the Allies entered Holland. The eager beavers were warned that freedom had not yet arrived, but it was at our doorstep.

So, here it was – at last!

Even with the good news about the Allies' approaching, it was sad watching many of the Germans, who had settled their families in the more prestigious homes—mostly Jewish homes—now piling their children and some essentials on a handcart, hoping to escape the approaching Allied forces. The bewilderment and hopelessness in their eyes and on their faces would even make the Devil feel pity. It was a long road ahead back to their homeland.

There was so much for us to celebrate, I thought. *Could we not share a little of our pity?* As it was, thoughts of them gave way to the business at hand.

What happened next was not easy to watch or forget.

The Amsterdam citizens, after much celebration, became hungry for revenge. They sought out the women who fraternized with the German soldiers. It didn't take long before half a dozen women had been found. These frightened women were told to climb on a large flatbed drawn by several horses. Not knowing what was going to happen to them, they begged for mercy. A mob gathered and jeered at them, paying no attention to their pleas. Five years of hidden frustration and suffering during the occupation seemed to have exploded that day. Their anger was taken out on these poor women. A frightening scene of hatred followed.

I stood quietly with my friend, Hank, watching this unreal scene of brutality. Many occupants of the apartment dwellings were eagerly watching the commotion going on below their open windows. One of the women on the flatbed looked up at a man above, in the building, and hollered, "You know I worked for the underground. Don't let this happen to me. Please!" Her pleading for help and understanding was in vain.

Hank and I watched as the horrible scene unfolded into something even more frightening. The women, whether guilty or not, were made to get on their knees. We watched in shock as their heads were shaved clean. Their frantic sobs were overshadowed with the hysterical chanting screams of bystanders. It became even more bizarre when their heads, now completely bald, were painted with red and orange and topped off with a black swastika. While this happened, the mob became even more excited. Their shouts were incomprehensible.

When this evil deed had been accomplished, the women were paraded on the horse-drawn flatbed through our neighborhoods. This was more than Hank and I could grasp. With the atrocious aftermath of falling bombs, cat fights in our night skies, death and destruction all around, the extreme hunger and numbing cold, and always-present fear of being arrested—all of that did not bring the evil of war so close to us as that dreadful day of reckoning on a rather lovely spring day in May 1945.

The corner bakery where Ada's mother bought the white bread for her family.

Chapter Seventeen

An Angel's Delight

After witnessing the awful ordeal put upon those poor women who were branded as traitors, put on the flatbed, and paraded through the streets, the only thought in my head was "HOME."

I wanted to be away from all this ugliness.

When I arrived, I found Mother in the backyard.

It was Monday, her laundry day, and she was busy taking her fresh wash off the lines before the chance of bad weather coming in could ruin it. She wrestled holding onto a huge pile of her washing from falling all over her feet. I couldn't help laughing at her for she looked so funny trying to keep this from happening.

She gave me a quick, "Oh, hello, Hopie. Give me a hand with this, okay? We will fold the laundry together." This surprised me because Mother had always been a fanatic about the way she liked her washing folded.

"Got to hurry," she said. "I've got a surprise for all of you, but not until it's supper time."

For a moment, I forgot my own problem I had to deal with and was reminded how much happier she was now that the war was over. The tears shed in the past, on an almost daily basis, were now replaced with gleeful smiles. It had only been a few months past when Father had burst into the front door of our home shouting, "*Lieverd,* where are you? The war is over. We just heard the news from the BBC!"

She interrupted those blissful memories when finally noticing my tear stained face, then asked, "What's wrong, Ada?"

The laundry was forgotten and my time with Mother had taken priority over good smelling, line-dried linens. After I told her what had happened, only a few blocks away from our home, it was her turn to wipe away tears, using one of Martin's undershirts. She murmured something I didn't understand, but the look in her eyes told me she did not agree with that kind of injustice.

After her sweet concern for my tender feelings and making sure the washing was folded, the table was set for a simple dinner. Oh, how wonderful that the vegetable man's stand was once again loaded with a variety of produce to choose from. Still on ration for most food items, at least, there was enough to go around for everyone. Much of our food still had to come from other sources, such as corned beef from the United States, material goods from Sweden, and so much more. The only food unfamiliar to us was corn from America. Corn, to the Dutch, was considered feed for animals and not meant for human consumption. The question was, "Do we eat this or feed it to chickens?"

"Well," Mother said. "We have no chickens. I do believe it is meant for us to eat it."

"I guess we had better warm it up first," Father suggested. "I'm sure it will taste better that way."

"Umm," Mother grumbled. "Hopefully, this will taste better than tulip bulbs."

The corn was boiled (probably too long), mustard was spread on it (butter was still rationed), and it tasted wonderful. There was also the surprise Mother had promised us. The table in our front room was cleaned off from the evening's meal dishes. The excitement of a pending surprise kept all of us in great suspense. Even Father must not have had any clue what Mother had in store for us. It became even more exciting when she placed her best Delft blue china dessert dishes in front of each one of us. Attention from all of us focused on the door going into the small kitchen, expecting her coming out with – who knew what? Sure enough, she came out carrying her matching Delft blue cake platter, placing it carefully in the middle of the table. It had been neatly covered with a square white and blue checkered dish towel.

"Papa," I whispered. "It smells like fresh bread." Father nodded in agreement. I could see the puzzled look on his face. He bent over a bit closer to me so he could hear me better. "Papa, is Mama going to serve us that horrible black looking bread the Nazis gave us to eat for dessert?"

His face became even more puzzled than before and answered, "Oh my, I hope not. There's enough to worry about. I would hate to think she has finally lost it."

Mother, being totally unaware of what we were whispering about, turned her attention to her curious, but worried family. Then, she hollered in a jubilant tone of voice, "Are you ready?"

"Of course we are!" Father shouted excitedly back at her.

Our mother pulled away the dish towel with a rather violent jerk and there to our surprise we were all staring at a delicious smelling huge loaf of all *white* bread. The reaction aroused by this magnificent-looking piece of culinary art was so loud even Hummus, who had been comfortable sleeping on Father's chair, jumped off and hid himself underneath the couch. When we all calmed down, we were each served with a thick slice of her wonderful white bread. Between every delicious bite, Mother told us that our neighborhood bakery, along with others, had been delivered white flour along with their usual wheat flour.

When our sweet Mama took her first bite of her portion of the white bread, she turned her eyes to Heaven and said, "It tastes as if an angel's peeing on my tongue. Amen!"

Ada... smiling from the heart.

Chapter Eighteen

Back to the Future

Many a wonderful meal followed that memorable dinner when we tasted white bread for the first time after the war. Mother's kitchen, once again, became a family meeting place. Her pots and pans were put to work on a regular basis.

Our cat, Hummus, who miraculously made it through "The Hunger Years," without ending her life in someone's Dutch oven, enjoyed the little treats from Mother's hand. Our much loved and very spoiled cat would smell the meat vendor blocks away selling meat scraps to his regular customers.

The owner of this enterprise stood no more than five-foot four-inches tall. The children around the neighborhood often made fun of the way he dressed. The baggy clothes he wore gave him a clown like appearance.

He'd holler with his high-pitched voice while casually pushing his vendor cart down the street shouting, "Love your pets. Buy my scraps."

No doubt, Mother was his best customer. The meat vendor's business grew rapidly as cats had to be imported from the Scandinavian countries into Holland. Most of the cat population ended up on the Nederlanders dinner table. The so-called "mouse problem" had become very intense because of the lack of our feline friends. Something needed to be done, but quickly. They finally arrived by the box loads from the Scandinavian countries—hundreds of cute, purring creatures. This invasion was not considered a problem, certainly not like the last one. So many changes happened at once.

The organ grinders appeared on the street scene, once more. Again, they added so much charm to our eight-hundred-year-old city.

To my own personal delight, the beloved puppet shows were again performed in front of the Royal Palace in Amsterdam—a tradition going back for decades. Punch and Judy were once more beating each other up.

The old market place recaptured its formal glory. The herring barrels, the pickle barrels, the colorful ribbons, notions and potions... goods of all kinds, helped to block out the ugliness of the past five years.

Mother ducks with their baby broods paddling right behind her were now undisturbed by German soldiers who'd used them as target practice.

Sirens, warning of approaching warplanes darkening our skies, had been put to rest.

Curfews were eliminated.

Back were the wonderful smells coming from the bakery shops.

The Allied soldiers, whether Americans, Canadians, or British, enjoyed their cups of coffee in the sidewalk cafes.

Also, there were exciting amphibious truck rides launching off into De Nassau Kade for a fun trip on the canal for only a nickel to the delight of the neighborhood children and adults alike.

Suddenly, our fair city had become a playground for both young and old. The Americans, Canadians, and British soldiers, with all their equipment that had come along with them, transformed Amsterdam. What was a city of gloom for the last five years of war, had now been turned into a lovely, lively place where the sun shined twenty-four a day, or so it seemed.

The city's heart had been lost for such a long time, but now it had all been given back to us, unfortunately at such a huge cost of lives.

An arduous and difficult task of rebuilding the many bombed-out ruins was now at hand. With financial foreign aid from the United States through something called "The Marshal Plan," the Dutch government did not let any grass grow underneath their feet. They started rebuilding right away. With great enthusiasm, this issue was certainly discussed at many a dinner table.

However, the conversation around our family dinner table went in a different direction. Plans had already been made by our parents to immigrate to the United States before the war broke out. Now, all this was discussed again. It had been our parents' desire to renew their marriage vows in the beautiful Salt Lake City, Utah, Mormon temple, for time and all eternity.

Father asked Mother, “Mama, can you take this adventure with me?”

Mothers answered bravely, “Why yes, I can do that. Give me a bowl, a spoon, and a few little miracles.”

We arrived in Utah in October 1949 and we were sealed as planned as an eternal family.

Lady Liberty welcomed the family to America.

Epilogue

OCTOBER 10, 1949

Preparations had been made for our family to immigrate to the United States. Hummus was taken in by Oma and Opa who stayed behind in the Netherlands, together with our brothers, Boy and Bobbie. Visas were in order and passports were together with all the legalities necessary to settle in a foreign country.

A very kind family living in California had agreed to sponsor us. We'd never met them personally, but they had been willing to take responsibility of our family if for some reason we needed assistance or support of any kind. Luckily, our family was physically well and financially our parents were prepared to take care of our needs. Father's brother's family had immigrated to the states several years before we did and was kind enough to share their home with us after we arrived for the time being.

Now, some years later, I look back at our departure from Holland.

The ship we traveled on was called "The New Amsterdam," a state-of-the-art luxury liner at the time. Father had booked us all for cabin class which had been overbooked. Fortunately, for us some of the cabin class passengers were placed in second class accommodations, including our family. Second class meant a shower in our cabin, room service, and, to our mother's delight, linen tablecloths on the dining room tables, as well as our very own waiter to take care of our needs.

One evening, when stuffed green peppers were listed on the dinner menu, our five-year-old sister, Nola, refused to eat any of it suspecting the green peppers actually were cooked frogs. Our sister's reaction to the stuffed green peppers still gets brought up in family get-togethers today. It had become one of mothers' favorite memories.

The weather and storms on the Atlantic Ocean in October could be frightful at times. We were told these huge storms weren't at all an unusual occurrence for that time of the year. As it so happened, we were caught right in the middle of experiencing one of the big October storms. These huge waves of water coming toward our ship made it feel as if we were going to be totally consumed by them. It was a fantastic sight to behold these huge powerful waves battering away at us. Our poor mother, however, had to deal with a bout of sea sickness. The rest of us coped rather well with the rough weather.

After ten days sailing, we were close to entering New York Harbor when our attention focused on the Statue of Liberty. Our mother was particularly excited because she had studied the history of Lady Liberty before we'd left Holland. An overwhelming feeling of anticipation took hold of all of us passing this world famous statue representing the freedom we had lost for a long time during the war years. It was an emotional encounter never to be forgotten.

We had finally arrived, setting foot in our new found country.

We left behind our beautiful ship, the linen tablecloths, the friendly waiter, the cozy cabin with the private shower, the great food and the cooked frogs. A small, ferry-type boat dropped us and many other passengers off at a place called Ellis Island.

My memory of this experience is somewhat limited with the exception of the excitement of the doctors and nurses. I remember the buzzing of eager immigrants from different countries with all of them speaking their own language. The windows were huge in this place, dwarfing everything below. It didn't take long after our physical exam that we took another ferry to the main land and boarded a Greyhound bus. The route the bus took us through was the backstreets of New York onto the highway. Traveling on a bus for three days with only occasional stops wasn't the best memory of our great adventure, but we made the most of it.

While passing through one of Chicago's streets, I spotted a young man and his wife pushing a baby buggy, obviously taking their precious baby out for some fresh air. What struck me as unusual was the young man was the one pushing the buggy. I had never seen that happen while growing up in the Netherlands. It simply wasn't done. This was considered the responsibility of the woman. I made up my mind right then and there, in old Chicago, that if those Yankee's didn't mind helping out by pushing a baby buggy, then I needed to marry me one of them... and... I did.

After this long arduous ride on the bus, we finally

arrived in Ogden, Utah, at the 24th Street Greyhound bus station. It was a busy street with lots of cars driving by. It was personally a great disappointment to me that driving by us were cars and not convoys of beautiful horses. After all, we were told by our American missionaries that folks in Utah rode horses. We had to accept that we did not land in the "wild west" after all, rather it was a beautiful, modern, mountainous city where people drive cars instead.

Soon after we arrived, Father's brother picked us up at the bus terminal. After less than a couple of months staying in our uncle's home, our parents bought their very first home in our new country. We became used to living in the new environment. Instead of being surrounded by canals and waterways like we had been in Amsterdam, we were bordered by the beautiful Rocky Mountains. It couldn't get better than that.

We were quickly introduced to Jell-O salads, casseroles, homemade bread, and barbeques. Around Thanksgiving time, the year after we arrived, Mother was given a ready-to-bake Thanksgiving turkey. Poor thing had no idea what she was looking at let alone how to prepare it. True to form, Mother got out her bowl and spoon. By some miracle, we feasted on a wonderful turkey dinner on our first celebrated holiday here in our new home.

Later on, we found out the home our parents bought in 1950 was the old Marcus Farr Home. His family was one of the early pioneers who had settled the Salt Lake valley in 1847. We were also told the Farr Home was the first brick house built in those early days of the pioneers. With all of this historic information, our home became even more special to us.

Because of the location of our home on Canyon Road, less than block away from the Loren Farr (a relative) stadium, we enjoyed a simulated historic moment on July

24th called Pioneer Day, commemorating the arrival of the Mormon pioneers in the valley. The occasion was celebrated when the rodeo folks came into town performing their "wild west" show in the stadium. At last, I finally got acquainted with handsome cowboys riding their beautiful horses.

Meanwhile, Father found a job working on the railroad. Mother worked several different jobs finally ending up as a nurse's aide in the operating room at McKay Dee Hospital in Ogden. She truly loved her job.

We came to love America the beautiful. As a family, we have grown in numbers as well as in spirit. The three things that brought us safely through the Nazi occupation were... our stubborn, positive Dutch attitude, our enduring faith, and our steadfast love for each other. Those things saved us again helping us during our perilous journey across the ocean and assisted us as we adapted to a new way of life in a new land.

We are truly grateful and blessed.

The Author

Today, Ada lives in Ogden, Utah, with her little dog, Max. She loves to knit and visit with her children, grandchildren, and friends.

Made in the USA
Columbia, SC
20 February 2020

88130409R00107